Living
Zealously

Deepen Your Christian Life

From the late 1500s to the early 1700s, Puritan ministers wrote thousands of Christian books that contain massive amounts of biblical, doctrinal, experiential, and practical instruction to energize and deepen your Christian life. During that period, thousands of volumes coming off English presses consisted of Puritan sermon material popularized in book form. Unfortunately, many believers today find it difficult to read the antiquarian Puritan language and, when they attempt to do so, find themselves more frustrated than energized.

This new series, Deepen Your Christian Life, presents in contemporary language the major teachings that several Puritans wrote on subjects that are seldom addressed adequately, if at all, today. Finally, you too will be able to enjoy the Puritans and experience, by the Spirit's grace, that they really do deepen your Christian life.

Living by God's Promises
    Joel R. Beeke and James La Belle (2010)

Living Zealously
    Joel R. Beeke and James La Belle (2012)

Living with a Good Conscience
    Joel R. Beeke (forthcoming)

Living Zealously

with Study Questions

Joel R. Beeke and James A. La Belle

Foreword by Derek W. Thomas

Reformation Heritage Books
Grand Rapids, Michigan

Reformation Heritage Books
2965 Leonard St. NE
Grand Rapids, MI 49525
616-977-0889 / Fax 616-285-3246
orders@heritagebooks.org
www.heritagebooks.org

Printed in the United States of America
12 13 14 15 16 17/10 9 8 7 6 5 4 3 2

Library of Congress Cataloging-in-Publication Data

Beeke, Joel R., 1952-
  Living zealously : with study questions / Joel R. Beeke and James A. La Belle ; foreword by Derek W.H. Thomas.
      p. cm. — (Deepen your Christian life)
   Includes bibliographical references (p.   ).
   ISBN 978-1-60178-179-6 (pbk. : alk. paper) 1. Enthusiasm—Religious aspects—Christianity—Textbooks. I. La Belle, James A. II. Title.
   BR112.B44 2012
   241'.4—dc23
                          2012010439

For additional Reformed literature, request a free book list from Reformation Heritage Books at the above regular or e-mail address.

Table of Contents

To

Joey Pipa

zealous puritan reformer and servant leader,
fellow seminary president and conference speaker,
loyal friend and brother in Christ for decades,
with whom I share so much in the gospel race

and

the dear flock of the

**Heritage Netherlands Reformed Congregation
in Grand Rapids, Michigan,**

in commemoration of having had the privilege of
serving you as a pastor for twenty-five years.

— JRB

⸺◆◆⸺

To
my dear children,

River, Schylie, Forrest, Terra, Sandy, Rocky, & Chantry,

the delight of a father's eyes,
the love of a father's heart,
the burden of a father's fervent prayers.

In a day when the zeal of the church has grown cold,
may God grant you the zeal of your gracious Savior
to overcome every sin,
pursue every virtue,
and take heaven by storm!

— JAL

Foreword

"Zeal is a subject, like many others in religion, most sadly misunderstood. Many would be ashamed to be thought 'zealous' Christians. Many are ready to say of zealous people what Festus said of Paul: 'They are beside themselves—they are mad' (Acts 26:24)." Thus wrote the nineteenth century Anglican Bishop of Liverpool, J. C. Ryle in a chapter entitled, "Zeal."[1] Several pages later, he made this observation: "It may be very true that wise young believers are very rare. But it is no less true that zealous old believers are very rare also."[2] That brings to me to this current volume on *Living Zealously* by Joel R. Beeke and James A. La Belle.

What Ryle observed a century ago is of even greater import in our own time: people are deeply suspicious of zeal (except, perhaps, in sports or entertainment). Think of the term "zealot" and what comes to mind? Fanaticism. Hatred. Bigotry. Add the descriptive "religious" to zeal and you have a verbal incendiary device. Whatever else it may mean, in the modern mind, such a thing is offensive. Thus, we encounter folk of choleric temperament, certain and robust, pushy and egoistic, determined to achieve their goal at whatever cost to those around them; intimidating, often *doing* and *speaking* in ways that appear to us excessively judgmental, narrow-minded, and offensive. Worse, a terrorist! Is this not how the world views zealous people, especially religiously zealous people? And the world is correct to be suspicious, at least, in some measure. Witness Paul's (or Saul's) own confession of his zeal in persecuting

---

1. J. C. Ryle, *Practical Religion* (Cambridge: James Clarke, 1970), 129.
2. Ryle, *Practical Religion,* 147.

the church (Phil. 3:6) and our suspicions are confirmed. He was out to kill people—zealously.

But "zeal" need not be such; channeled in the right direction, with accompanying grace, zeal is a fruit of the Spirit's sanctifying work. It is an expression of devotion, single-minded determination to please God and fellow human beings. Thus Paul again, commending Corinthian Christian repentance (2 Cor. 7:11), or Roman Christian industry (Rom. 12:11), advances zeal as laudable and commendatory. Here, zeal is humble, reverent, God-focused, aware of others but resolute to serve God with one's entire self. Listen to Ryle again:

> A zealous man in religion is pre-eminently a man of one thing. It is not enough to say that he is earnest, hearty, uncompromising, thorough-going, whole-hearted, fervent in spirit. He only sees one thing, he cares for one thing, he lives for one thing, he is swallowed up in one thing; and that one thing is to please God. Whether he lives, or whether he dies—whether he is rich, or whether he is poor—whether he pleases men, or whether he gives offence—whether he is thought wise, or whether he is thought foolish—whether he gets honour, or whether he gets shame—for all this the zealous man cares nothing at all. He burns for one thing; and that one thing is, to please God, and to advance God's glory.[3]

Such a thing, of course, will never appeal to the world, nor, sadly, to lukewarm Christians. But it is what Jesus expects of us and what the gospel encourages. It is this kind of zeal, one that is focused on giving God glory whatever the cost to oneself, that Beeke and La Belle, gleaning from the riches of the Puritans, commend in this book. It is *godly* zeal. It is Christ-centered, gospel-infused zeal. Would you not have such a thing characterize your love for Christ? Then read on....

Derek W. H. Thomas
Minister of Preaching and Teaching,
   First Presbyterian Church, Columbia
Professor of Systematic and Historical
   Theology, RTS

---

3. Ryle, *Practical Religion,*130.

Biographical Introduction

This book draws from Puritan writers on the subject of zeal—the inflaming of our heart to pant after God's glory and to pursue His will with all our might. Puritans such as William Ames, Oliver Bowles, John Evans, Richard Greenham, Christopher Love, John Reynolds, and Samuel Ward[1] thoroughly addressed this theme, so seldom addressed today. Their work is featured in this book. Here is a brief introduction to these pastor-theologians.

William Ames (1576–1633)

William Ames was born in 1576 in Ipswich, Suffolk. Both his parents died when he was young. His uncle raised him in a family deeply committed to Puritan ideals. Ames obtained his bachelor of arts (1598) and master of arts (1601) degrees from Christ's College, Cambridge University. While completing his degrees, he experienced a personal conversion after realizing that a person may be moral without being godly. After graduation he was elected fellow[2] at the college and ordained into ministry in the Church of England. Ames had a profound spiritual and academic influence at the college for several years.

---

1. The Ames, Greenham, and Love sections of this introduction are adapted from Joel R. Beeke and Randall J. Pederson, *Meet the Puritans, with a Guide to Modern Reprints* (Grand Rapids: Reformation Heritage Books, 2006), 39–51, 290–96, 396–403.

2. In English universities, a fellow was a graduate of a particular college, elected as an incorporated member of the college, with appropriate rank and privileges. Many fellows had teaching and tutoring responsibilities.

King James I and some of the Anglican bishops made life increasingly difficult for the Puritans. In 1609 Ames resigned from his Cambridge fellowship, and soon found himself banned from preaching by the bishop of London. The next year he sought greater freedom in the Netherlands, where he remained for the rest of his life.

From 1611 to 1619 he served as a chaplain to the English military forces in The Hague. He simultaneously labored as the pastor of a small congregation. His writings against the Arminian Remonstrants gave him the title "the Augustine of Holland." This led to his role as a nonvoting advisor to the presiding officer of the Synod of Dort, where an international group of Reformed theologians issued the famous Five Points affirming divine sovereignty in salvation.

The powers of England forced Ames out of his chaplaincy and closed the door for him to teach at Leiden University, so he tutored university students in his study for three years to support his family. His lectures to students later developed into his *Marrow of Theology*. In 1622 Franeker University appointed him as professor of theology. There Ames again turned his home into a tutoring center for theological and moral formation. Students from all over Europe came to study under him. However, opposition from several professors, together with declining health, led him to move once again.

He went to Rotterdam in the summer of 1633 to serve with Hugh Peter as the pastor of English refugees and to start a new college. But that fall the Maas River flooded his house, which negatively impacted his health, leading to his death from pneumonia at age fifty-seven. His books, such as the theological masterpiece, *Marrow*, and his ethical work, *Conscience*, profoundly shaped the Reformed movement in Europe, Britain, and New England for more than a century.

Oliver Bowles (c. 1577–c. 1644)

Oliver Bowles was born around 1577 in Sawtry, Huntingdonshire. He taught at Queens College, Cambridge, from 1599 to 1606, where he tutored such leading Puritans as John Preston, who regarded him as "a holy and learned man." He then served many years as a pastor at Sutton in Bedfordshire.

Bowles was an elder member of the Westminster Assembly but died before it finished its work. He preached before Parliament on a fast day commemorating the opening of the assembly on the topic of zeal, from which this book draws. He faithfully attended the proceedings of the assembly, but we have no records of his playing a major role in its deliberations.

After Bowles died, his son published his only book, *De Pastore Evangelico Tractatus* ("A Treatise on the Evangelical Pastor"). This four-hundred-page Latin treatise expands on almost every pastoral duty listed in the Westminster Directory for Public Worship, providing a practical Puritan description of the office of a shepherd. In this book Bowles frequently quoted the Reformers and leaders of the early church, reflecting the historical roots of Puritanism.[3]

John Evans (c. 1680–1730)

John Evans was born around 1680 in Wrexham, northern Wales, the son of multiple generations of ministers. His father was ejected from his ministry by the Act of Uniformity but continued to serve a congregation in Wrexham. John studied for the ministry in private schools, reading through, it is said, all five massive volumes of Matthew Poole's Latin *Synopsis Criticorum aliorumque Sacrae Scripturae*.

Evans was ordained to the ministry in 1702 in Wrexham, where he served until 1704. Daniel Williams then invited him to serve with him in London, and in 1716 he succeeded Williams. Both the universities of Edinburgh and Aberdeen awarded him a doctorate in divinity. He was a leader among the Dissenters and a favorite choice to preach at their public meetings. He also lectured for several years at Salters' Hall.

Matthew Henry assisted at Evans's ordination. After Henry's death, Evans completed the notes on Romans included in Henry's famous

---

3. Philip G. Ryken, "Oliver Bowles and the Westminster View of Gospel Ministry," in *The Westminster Confession into the Twenty-First Century, Volume 2* (Ross-shire, U.K.: Christian Focus Publications, 2004), 410–14.

commentary. Isaac Watts and Philip Doddridge considered Evans's *Practical Discourses Concerning the Christian Temper* to be one of the best treatises on practical Christianity. He planned to write a comprehensive history of nonconformity in the sixteenth and seventeenth centuries, but ill health ended his life before he could.

He died in his fifty-first year from dropsy and other medical problems, which were aggravated by the stress of financial difficulties. His library of ten thousand volumes was sold at auction to provide for the needs of his widow and children.

Richard Greenham (c. 1542–1594)

Richard Greenham was a pioneer in Puritan pastoral ministry. He graduated with a bachelor of arts degree from Pembroke Hall in Cambridge, then earned a master's degree in 1567, and became a fellow at the school. In 1570 he began serving as pastor in a small agricultural village, Dry Dayton, five miles from Cambridge. The people there had little interest in the things of God.

Greenham devoted himself to the ministry, preaching twice on Sundays and rising at 4:00 a.m. to preach on four weekdays. His preaching was so earnest that he often drenched himself in sweat. He sought to build a foundation of knowledge in his people by catechizing them on Thursdays and Sunday afternoons, using his adaptation of the Anglican catechism with many questions and short answers. He also called people to keep the Sabbath holy.

His fame grew as a wise spiritual counselor who broke new ground in Puritan "casuistry" or application of the Bible to specific practical questions. He trained several men for the ministry in his own home, including Arthur Hildersam and Henry Smith. He also organized local charitable projects to provide food for the poor.

When Greenham left Dry Dayton in 1591, he grieved that he did not see more fruit on his ministry of more than two decades there. He went to London and stayed there to serve people in preaching and visitation. In 1593 the plague erupted. Greenham died a year later, perhaps not from the plague but rather from a combination of other medical problems. His *Works* were published in 1599 and read by many.

Christopher Love (1618–1651)

Christopher Love was born in Cardiff, Wales, in 1618, and God converted him while he was in his teens. He graduated from New Inn Hall, Oxford, with a bachelor of arts degree in 1639. His studies for a master's degree were interrupted by persecution against the Puritans. He refused to subscribe to Archbishop Laud's rules in 1640, and was imprisoned in 1641. From prison he preached through the bars to large crowds of people. In 1642 he served as chaplain to the Parliamentary regiment under John Venn.

Love was ordained as a Presbyterian preacher in 1645 in London. He was a member of the Westminster Assembly but did not participate much in it. In 1652 Oliver Cromwell's forces arrested him for his alleged participation in a plot to restore Charles II to the throne of England. Despite the appeals of his wife and several ministers, he was sentenced to death and beheaded. In his prayer prior to his death, he cried out, "O that London might be a faithful city to Thee!" His last words were, "Blessed be God for Jesus Christ."

Thomas Manton preached Love's funeral sermon to a large crowd of mourners. His wife wrote a memoir of him, and fifteen volumes of his sermons were published posthumously.

John Reynolds (1667–1727)

John Reynolds was born in 1667, in Wolverhampton, Staffordshire. His father, a minister, medical doctor, and friend of Richard Baxter, was ejected from his ministry in 1661. Reynolds received ordination as a dissenting minister in 1699, serving as a family chaplain from 1699 to 1706. Then he worked as a co-pastor with James Forbes at Gloucester.

In 1708 he was given charge of a dissenting church and school in Shrewsbury. He also lectured in Dudley, where in 1715 a mob of rioters shouted threats at "the little Presbyterian parson." Sickness forced him to leave Shrewsbury in 1718, and in 1721 he moved to Walsall to work as an assistant pastor until he died in 1727.

In addition to his book on zeal, Reynolds published a catechism for adults and a sermon lamenting the death of Matthew Henry. He also contributed to a book that defended the doctrine of the Trinity.

Samuel Ward (1577–1640)

Samuel Ward was born in 1577, in Suffolk, where his father served as pastor. He received his bachelor of arts degree from St. John's College, Cambridge, in 1597, and his master's degree in 1600. He lectured at Haverhill, where the Lord used him in the conversion of Samuel Fairclough. Ward had preached about the necessity of repentance and restitution, and Fairclough was pierced to the heart because of his recent theft of fruit from a local orchard. He could find no peace for his corrupt heart until he obtained the forgiveness of the orchard owner, and, through Ward's counsel, the forgiveness of God through Jesus Christ.

In 1603 Ward was called to serve as the preacher in the wealthy town of Ipswich, which was a great honor for a twenty-six-year-old man. He ministered there for three decades, and his preaching had a magnetic influence.

Ward's nonconformity brought him under legal prosecution in 1622. He came under censure in 1635 and was imprisoned. He went to Holland and served as a pastor briefly with William Bridge. By 1638 he returned to Ipswich, where he died in 1640. He was so respected that the town continued to pay his stipend to his widow and son.

He published several works over his lifetime, including *A Coal from the Altar to Kindle the Holy Fire of Zeal*, which went through four editions from 1615–1622, and appeared again in a collection of sermons printed in 1628 and 1636, and was reprinted in 1862, edited by J. C. Ryle.

Contemporary Style

We have footnoted direct quotations from these seven authors. Much of the other material in the book summarizes their thoughts in a contemporary form. We have also used other Puritan authors to augment our theme of living zealously; they are footnoted in full. Modern spelling and punctuation are used throughout, except in book titles. Study questions are offered at the end of each chapter to facilitate group study.

Acknowledgments

Our heartfelt gratitude is again extended first and foremost to our great triune God, who is zealous for His glory and His people's salvation. We would also like to thank our dear wives, Mary Beeke and Chantry La Belle, for their amazing loyalty to us, and to our patient and loving children (Calvin, Esther, and Lydia Beeke; River, Schylie, Forrest, Terra, Sandy, Rocky, and Chantry La Belle). Many thanks to Derek W. Thomas for his helpful foreword to this volume. Thanks, too, to Phyllis Ten Elshof, Rev. Ray Lanning, and Rev. Paul Smalley for their helpful editing and proofing assistance, and to Gary and Linda den Hollander, our excellent proofreading/typesetting team, as well as Amy Zevenbergen for the cover design.

If this book helps to enable God's dear children to be more zealous for His glory, the salvation of the lost, and the maturity of the saints, our labor will be well rewarded.

—Joel R. Beeke and James A. La Belle

Abbreviations

Ames   William Ames, "Of Zeale," in *Conscience with the Power and Cases Thereof* (n.p., 1639), 56–60 [book 3, ch. 6].

Bowles   Oliver Bowles, *Zeale for Gods House quickned: or, A sermon preached before assembly of Lord, Commons, and Divines, at their solemn fast Iuly 7, 1643* (London: by Richard Bishop for Samuel Gellibrand, 1643).

Evans   John Evans, "Christian Zeal," Sermon XVIII, in *Practical Discourses Concerning the Christian Temper* (London: for C. and R. Ware, T. Longman, and J. Johnson, 1773).

Greenham   Richard Greenham, "Of Zeal," a sermon from "Seven Godlie and Frvitfvll Sermons Vpon Svndry Portions of Holy Scripture," in *The Workes of the Reverend and faithfvll servant of Iesus Christ, M. Richard Greenham, Minister and Preacher of the word of God* (London: Imprinted by Felix Kingston for Ralph Iacson, 1599), 113–20.

Love   Christopher Love, *The Zealous Christian: Taking Heaven by Holy Violence In Wrestling and Holding Communion with God in Importunate Prayer* (repr., Morgan, Pa.: Soli Deo Gloria, 2002).

Reynolds   John Reynolds, *Zeal a Virtue: or, A Discourse Concerning Sacred Zeal* (London: Printed for John Clark, 1716).

Ward   Samuel Ward, "A Coal from the Altar to Kindle the Holy Fire of Zeal," in *Sermons and Treatises* (Edinburgh: Banner of Truth, 1996), 69–91.

Setting the Stage:
An Appeal for Zeal

How long shall we lie still under our formal complaints of the *decay* of Christian piety? How long shall we idly see the *retirement* of warm religion from the hearts and bosoms of its professors? Do we look into the *churches* of the Lord Jesus, or into our own *souls* and observe the deadness and dispiritedness that is there to all the parts of real godliness; and are we content, that so it should be? Are we willing to yield to all the lukewarmness and degeneracy that has overspread us? Shall we take no methods to recover and revive?

So begins John Reynolds's *Zeal a Virtue, or a Discourse Concerning Sacred Zeal*, published in 1716. Reynolds continues, "[Even] the truly pious are dull and heavy in their religion, [and] march on weariedly in their appointed race, as if either their Lord had lost His glory or His promise to them; or they [have lost] their faith and hope in Him."[1]

Do these words stab our hearts? Who among us cannot see the difference between the early church and our churches, between the apostles and ourselves, between the Reformers and Puritans of several hundred years ago and those of us who claim to be their heirs today? A fire burned in their hearts, but are we aflame at all? They seemed driven by a holy passion and resolve, but little seems to motivate us. They were at war with their sin and pursued holiness as if empowered by heavenly strength, but we are too much at peace with our sins and content to do little more than the minimum that God requires of us. Why is there such a difference between them and us?

---

1. Reynolds, 1–2.

The Call for Christian Zeal

God has not changed since the time of the Reformers and Puritans. The power of God unto salvation has not changed, the call to holiness has not changed, the threat of the enemy has not changed, but something has indeed changed. Furthermore, something is missing both in the church and in the hearts of the majority of Christians. That something is *zeal*. We lack zeal for God's honor and glory (1 Cor. 10:31), zeal for God's house and God's Word (Pss. 69:9; 119:139), zeal for the advance of Christ's kingdom (1 Cor. 9:19–23), zeal for repentance and good works (Rev. 3:19; Titus 2:14), zeal to "cut off" the offending hand and "pluck out" the offending eye (Mark 9:43–48), zeal for that "holiness, without which no man shall see the Lord" (Heb. 12:14), zeal that overcomes all obstacles and perseveres to the end (1 Cor. 9:24–27).

Christian zeal is the divine flame that brings our affections to a boil for God's cause. It enlivens and compels us, stirs and empowers us, and directs and governs us as it sets our affections ablaze for the glory of God and the good of His church. Zeal is "an earnest desire of and concern for all things pertaining to the glory of God and Kingdom of the Lord Jesus among men."[2]

Think about it. If all Christians by God's grace are indwelt by the Spirit of God, and if all Christians have the seed of regeneration alive within them, then what is it but zeal that causes one believer to differ from another in passion, desire, affection, devotion, sacrifice, and fervor? It is true that not all believers have the same capacity. All have not received the same measure or degree of grace and faith (Rom. 12:3, 6; 14:1); the Spirit does not work to the same degree in all (1 Cor. 12:11). Zeal is what makes us, who are otherwise essentially the same, differ in the outworking and fruitfulness of our common salvation. Samuel Ward wrote, "What makes one Christian differ from another in grace, as stars do in glory, but zeal? All believers have a like precious faith; all true Christians have all graces in their seeds; but the degrees of them are no way better discerned than by zeal."[3] Do we not appreciate and love the Christian whose life so sweetly, harmoniously, and passionately

---

2. Reynolds, 18.
3. Ward, 78.

displays sacred zeal? And are we not troubled by the Christian whose life displays carelessness and indifference toward the things of God, who cares not whether he grows in grace or puts off sin, but is satisfied with a mediocre, half-baked discipleship?

We should examine ourselves to determine the quality, measure, and temperature of our own sacred zeal. It would be foolish to assume, as did the Laodiceans, that we are "rich, and increased with goods, and have need of nothing," when, upon a searching examination, we might prove to be "wretched, and miserable, and poor, and blind, and naked" (Rev. 3:17). Furthermore, if sacred zeal is what sets a Christian ablaze for the glory of God and assists us in subduing sin, then we should be diligent to consider what this zeal is and by what means we might secure and sustain it.

We will examine Christian zeal so that we might understand it and, by God's grace, be possessed by it. The Puritans wrote and preached much upon this matter, encouraging the saints to "be zealous...and repent" (Rev. 3:19), to put on "zeal as a cloak" (Isa. 59:17), to be consumed with zeal for the Lord's house (Ps. 69:9; John 2:17), and to be "zealous of good works" (Titus 2:14). We will draw from their writings and sermons to provide instruction for our own day.

Christian Zeal and Its Critics

We live in a day when the visible church is sick with spiritual lethargy, dullness, and presumption; a day when few understand or display Christian zeal; a day when many are ablaze with blind and false zeal; and a day when what passes for Christian fruitfulness is really little more than foliage. One wonders whether the axe is even now laid at the root of the tree of the modern church because of its lack of zeal. How much longer will the Lord of the vineyard wait for our fruit before He calls the dresser of the vineyard to reach for the axe and says, "Cut it down" (Matt. 3:7–10; 21:18–19; Luke 13:6–9)?

May God see fit in His mercy to use this book as a means to awaken His church from her slumber and fill her members with a Christian zeal, so that the world will once again be compelled to say of them that "they

[have] been with Jesus," and will have no other charge to lay against them than that they "have turned the world upside down" (Acts 4:13; 17:6)!

Some critics have objected to sacred zeal, calling it a rash and heady temper that hurts more than it helps, and a harsh and fiery spirit that blindly burns up everything in its path. It is strange, however, that those who argue against sacred zeal are themselves zealous, maybe not about those things for which they despise zeal in others, but for those things that they themselves love. Their zeal could be for a political persuasion, a favorite sports team, the reputation of being a winner, making money, or being the best dressed. Whatever it is, it is safe to say that we are *all* zealous about something (and in most cases, about many things) when we love it enough to make considerable, if not foolish, sacrifices pursuing it. So zeal itself is not truly being opposed, is it? We all understand what zeal is, and, in one way or another, practice it toward what we most love or want.

While it is true that we are all zealous *for* what we most love and want, it is just as true that we are all zealous *against* what we most hate and reject. For example, if we love one political party, we tend to hate the other. If the party that we hate wins an election, is not our zeal set ablaze against those who support that party, so that we decry their policies, slander their candidates, and mock their promises? You see, zeal operates both *for* what we love and *against* what we hate. We are all enflamed by some kind of zeal and therefore should not oppose it in others. For the most part, we do make allowances for others' zeal and passion. We respect their positions and simply agree to disagree. Having said that, why are so many people opposed to Christian zeal? Should there not be zeal in Christianity?

Given that the Christian religion is the means by which we worship God, enjoy reconciliation and communion with Him, and receive His blessings, should not we be truly zealous in our Christianity? It has been said, "In other objects fear excess; here no ecstasy is high enough."[4] We acknowledge, of course, that false zeal can easily take things too far, and does so whenever it exceeds the boundaries of God's Word. False zeal

---

4. Ward, 77.

can be wrong in significantly different ways: in some cases, it can be violent or hateful; in other cases it can be sincere, albeit misguided, such as in those instances when a person in the name of the sanctity of human life bombs abortion clinics or murders doctors who perform abortions.

But why should we condemn someone aflame with true Bible-based zeal by calling him a fanatic or a radical who "takes things too far"? Or, when someone questions us about an inconsistency between what we preach and what we practice, why must we offer a litany of excuses about why it is better to walk a more moderate path and not go overboard with religion? Sadly, many Christians wonder if the sacred zeal that consumed Christians in the past is necessary today and will even argue for moderation as the wiser and more practical course in religion.

How can this tide be turned? How can the pretense of moderation behind which so much sinful compromise hides be purged? How can the hearts of today's slumbering and drifting Christians be enlivened with true zeal for God? How can the flame of zeal in the hearts of God's people be fanned until they are ablaze with love for God and His house?

How can we expose and cut off blind and rash zeal, while, by grace, stirring up in God's people a directed, resolute, and purposed Christian zeal *against* all things sinful and *for* all things holy? On the one hand, we must clear Christian zeal of false charges, while on the other, we must lift up Christian zeal in all its glory and beauty. Once we see the virtue of true Christian zeal and feel its heat and know its blessings, who among us would not plead with God to give us this zeal and set us ablaze for His cause?

In this book, we will do our best to help you understand what Christian zeal is, and encourage you to be consumed with it for the glory of God, His church, and His Word, as were David and Christ (Pss. 69:9; 119:139; John 2:17). In chapter 1 we will speak of the nature and marks of Christian zeal, in contrast to a false and blind zeal. Many people are perishing today because of blind zeal, even in their religion. Having cleared the way for true zeal, we will move on in chapter 2 to explain the necessity of true Christian zeal and urge you to begin asking God for it. Chapter 3 will lay out the rule by which godly zeal is governed in its course, and answer objections against zeal. Chapter 4 will encourage you to maintain a consistent zeal by describing several ways in which a Christian zeal expresses itself. In chapter 5 we will further pursue that same theme, adding some of the fruits and benefits of Christian zeal in several spheres of life. Finally, so that you might truly, practically, and sincerely enjoy sacred zeal, chapter 6 will show the means by which you may obtain and maintain it.

The Nature and Marks
of Christian Zeal

Christian zeal is not easy to describe, especially at a time when we see and hear so little of it. Furthermore, what little we hear about it is dominated by critics who despise and mock it. When did you last hear a sermon or take part in a Bible study on Christian zeal? So let us begin this study by considering the nature and character of Christian zeal.

The Nature of Christian Zeal

Many people have confused true Christian zeal, to which the Lord calls His people, with the blind and rash fervor of someone who is ignorant, uneven, inconsistent, and hypocritical. This confused zeal is admittedly damaging, not only to the person ablaze with it since he runs feverishly after the wrong things, but also to the cause of Christ, which sets true zeal aflame within believers. A blind and rash zeal misrepresents the beauty of God's people who are on fire for the Lord. Therefore let us be clear about the nature of true Christian zeal.

The first thing to note about Christian zeal is that it is a purposeful stirring and enflaming of the affections. It is a holy passion, which, like a magnifying glass that concentrates the sun's rays into a single point of light, captures the believer's affections and drives them towards a specific, biblical goal. In his sermon on Revelation 3:19, Samuel Ward said zeal is neither a degree or intention of love, nor any other single affection, nor even a mixed affection, but instead is "a hot temper, higher degree or intention of them all. [Just as] varnish is no one color, but that which gives gloss and luster to all, [and as] the opposites of zeal, key-coldness[1] and lukewarmness…are no affections, but several tempers of them all."[2] Likewise, Samuel Annesley (1620–1696), in his Cripplegate sermon on Matthew 22:37–38, said that zeal is "the boiling-up of the affections to the greatest heat."[3] And John Evans, also preaching on Revelation 3:19, argued that zeal "is not a particular grace or virtue by itself, but rather a qualification which should attend us in the exercise of grace, and in the performance of every duty."[4]

Simply defined, a truly zealous person is one whose fervency and passion have enflamed all his affections towards an object: "his love is ever fervent, his desires eager, his delights ravishing, his hopes longing, his hatred deadly, his anger fierce, his grief deep, his fear terrible."[5] This is not a simple zeal by which the affections burn for or against an object that happens to suit its fancy at a particular time. Rather, true Christian zeal is ignited by fire from heaven like Elijah's offering on Mount Carmel (1 Kings 18:36–39), and therefore directs all affections to a holy and God-honoring end, the greater glory of God, and the good of His church.

John Reynolds wrote of zeal as being "of considerable latitude and extent…set in opposition to lukewarmness" in the letter of Christ to the church of Laodicea in Revelation 3.[6] This means that the nature of zeal can be seen not only in its own light, but also in the light of what is contrary to it: lukewarmness, neither hot nor cold. According to Reynolds, "Lukewarmness may be justly supposed the disease of the whole soul; the *deliquium* [declension],[7] the faintness and debility of the whole new nature; the things that remain may be ready to die. Lukewarmness

---

1. *Webster's* defines *key-cold* as "cold as a metal key; devoid of the warmth of life; apathetic and indifferent."

2. Ward, 72.

3. Samuel Annesley, "How May We Attain to Love God with All Our Hearts, Souls, and Minds?" *Puritan Sermons, 1659–1689* (Wheaton, Ill.: Richard Owen Roberts, 1981), 1:616.

4. Evans, 320.

5. Ward, 72.

6. Reynolds, 14.

7. The Latin word *deliquium* means want or defect, the lack of something needful; *Webster's* says it is "a failure of vitality, or what in infants and young children is termed a failure to thrive."

will not barely be the defect of any one single grace or Christian virtue, but the lethargy and benumbedness of every one. [It is] the universal languor of the soul toward God and religion."[8]

Sacred zeal, which is diametrically opposed to lukewarmness, is not "merely the vigor of any one grace, or spiritual endowment, but the vivacity and strength of every one."[9] Reynolds suggested that in relation to all the affections that it encompasses, zeal can be compared "with that subordinate virtue of sincerity. Or, you may [even] call it sincerity advanced to a rich and noble degree. For sincerity is not a single or distinct grace, or sacred virtue of itself, but the reality and truth of every grace. It runs, like a metaphysical affection, through all the holy dispositions of the soul and gives a denomination to them all. So zeal (being accumulated sincerity) will affect and denominate the sacred affections and virtues likewise. Zeal will quicken all the active dispositions at once."[10] Sacred zeal is "the vigor and ardency of the renewed, consecrated soul. 'Tis divine grace, bubbling up in the heart, and flowing out into the life and practice…the effervescence of inward grace, the warmed emotion of a religious soul."[11]

In addition, when speaking from Matthew 11:12 of the holy violence of affection whereby men press[12] into the kingdom of God (cf. Luke 16:16), Love described sacred zeal as a violence "opposed to lukewarmness in religion, to that coldness and frozenness that is in the hearts of men under the preaching of the Word."[13] When asked about the nature of this holy violence, Love said it is "a full and vehement vent of a man's desires, affections, and endeavors after Jesus Christ in the gospel, so that no difficulties or discouragements whatsoever shall take him off from his pursuit after Christ in the way of His ordinances."[14]

In preaching before the Westminster Assembly on John 2:17, Oliver Bowles urged the delegates to seek from God "such a frame of spirit,

---

8. Reynolds, 14–15.
9. Reynolds, 15.
10. Reynolds, 15.
11. Reynolds, 15–16.
12. Young's *Analytical Concordance*: "to force, use force."
13. Love, 3.
14. Love, 22.

such an assistance from on high, such a clear light, as may rise us above ourselves, fit us for that work whereunto we have no sufficiency as from ourselves."[15] It was a sermon based on Christ's own example, according to John 2:17, in seeking from God the "utmost zeal" that was necessary for the work of reforming the church.

Bowles said that zeal "is a holy ardor kindled by the Holy Spirit of God in the affections, improving a man to the utmost for God's glory, and the Church's good.... It is not so much any one affection, as the intended degree of all."[16] In other words, zeal raises the affections to the point that a person rallies every faculty and strength to press into the kingdom (Luke 16:16). Bowles added, "What the wheels are to the cart, the sinews to the body, wings to the bird, the wind to the sails spread, such are the affections to the soul, implanted by God to carry it hither and thither as the objects do more or less affect [i.e., draw out the affections]. Man lies like a log; the soul moves not, but as the affections stir."[17]

So by nature Christian zeal is the grace that invigorates and inflames all our affections toward a sole purpose and, more specifically, a holy purpose. It is the gracious propensity given to the soul by the Spirit of God that incites and inclines all our affections toward God and His kingdom.[18] It is the divine grace that enables the once barren affections to bring forth the fruits of righteousness in every area of life. Without it, we would make our way to the kingdom at a snail's pace. Rather than taking heaven by a storm of holy violence,[19] we carry on as if someone will run the race for us; rather than burning with a desire for Christ that refuses to be denied or put off, our affections are as good as asleep, flowing thick and heavy within and hardly moved by anything without. May God rid us of lukewarmness and grant us this fiery zeal.

---

15. Bowles, 4.
16. Bowles, 5–6.
17. Bowles, 6.
18. Reynolds, 14.
19. Cf. Thomas Watson, *Heaven Taken by Storm, Showing the Holy Violence a Christian is to Put Forth in the Pursuit after Glory,* ed. Joel R. Beeke (Morgan, Pa.: Soli Deo Gloria, 1992).

The Marks of Christian Zeal

Christian zeal is distinguished by its characteristics, or identifying marks. Where these fruits are found, either in us or others, we can be sure that sacred zeal is at the root; where these characteristics are absent, whatever a person might claim, true zeal is missing. Now that we have some idea of the nature of Christian zeal, we can consider its characteristics to determine whether we burn with this heavenly fire. Since zeal is that divine grace that awakens and inclines all the affections for God, there are many properties that explain how this root will bear its many fruits.

1. Christian zeal is marked by love for God. Because both the author and object of Christian zeal is the living God, the zealous Christian is possessed with a fervent love for God that craves God's presence, grieves when God's name and cause suffer injury, and is indignant toward those who oppose and obstruct God's honor.

The zealous Christian is pleased with the tokens of love he enjoys in God's absence, but he longs for the fullest enjoyment of God's presence in His house. Reynolds said, "It pleads the beauties of His face, the pleasures of His presence, and cries out, 'When shall I appear before God in Zion?'"[20] This zeal creates a hunger and thirst for God, and an impatient desire to be with Him. It makes the Christian "look out of [his] casements and cry out, why are His chariots so long in coming?" Reynolds continued. "He is ready to say to the traveling angels…'I charge you that when you see my Beloved, you tell Him that I am sick with love.' Yea, he pours out his soul in panting desires to his Lord Himself, 'Come, Lord Jesus! Come quickly! Come, and take me to Thyself! And fill me with Thy presence, and satiate me with Thy love!'"[21]

This fervent love for God also awakens grief in the zealous soul when God's name and cause are injured. For while the zealous soul knows that no real hurt can be done to the Almighty, he is mindful of God's dignity and prerogatives. Like David in Psalm 119:136–139, the zealous soul mourns whenever God's rights are violated. It grieves him

---

20. Reynolds, 41.
21. Reynolds, 41–42.

to see the Lovely One so little loved, the Adorable One so little adored, the Creator forgotten by creatures made in His own image, the Universal Governor ignored by His people, to see His laws trampled upon, His Word despised, His house neglected, His name abused, and the Lord of glory crucified every day and put to an open shame.[22] "How can they choose but lament, as long as they live in such a world as this?" Reynolds asked.[23] "Zeal for the Great God must needs issue into consuming grief for the rampant indignities offered to His rights and government."[24]

So fervent love leads to righteous anger. As anger is ascribed both to the Father and the Son in Scripture (Num. 11:33; Ps. 2:12), we should not be surprised that anger is also found in the zealous soul in whom the triune God resides. Reynolds wrote, "*Sacred zeal*, while militant, must needs put on the habit of *anger* and *wrath*. It has opposers to grapple with, difficulties to remove; obstructions thrown in the way of its duty and desire, to surmount and overcome. The cause and honor of its Beloved is to be patronized and vindicated against adversaries and rivals. And how shall this be done without some angry resentment of the indignities and offenses of those foolish adversaries?"[25] We see this holy anger in Phineas (Num. 25:6–8), Moses (Ex. 32:19–20), Peter (Acts 8:20–21), and Paul (Acts 17:16); we should therefore expect that "upon some emergencies, zeal for one person or thing puts on the form of *anger* towards another."[26]

2. Christian zeal is ruled by Scripture. As opposed to that false zeal for God to which Paul refers in Romans 10:2, sacred zeal is *according to knowledge* and therefore kept within the compass of the rule of Scripture. Beveridge wrote, "For no zeal for His honor can justify any breach of His laws. And as it is 'good to be zealously affected always in a good thing' [Gal. 4:18], it is a good thing only for which we should be ever so affected. Not for any private opinion, not for a party or faction, not

---

22. Reynolds, 37.
23. Reynolds, 37.
24. Reynolds, 38.
25. Reynolds, 39. Cf. John 2:17; Numbers 25:6–8.
26. Reynolds, 39.

for either side of a doubtful disputation, nor for unwritten traditions, wherein men are apt to spend all their zeal, so as to have little or none left for that which is the proper object of it."[27]

If we are to honor and serve God, whom we fervently love in zeal, we must know what His will and good pleasure are. That requires us to have constant regard for His Word. The Jewish zeal referred to in Romans 10:2 was zeal for God, but it fell short of being sacred zeal because it knew nothing of the knowledge of God's righteousness (v. 3), which the Jews should have known from the Word itself (Rom. 10:6–8). Christian zeal is founded on and consecrated to knowledge of the truth, for the Holy Spirit, with the grace of zeal, brings a suitable view of God and His cause into the heart so that when the affections are inflamed, they understand the channel in which they are to flow. Such knowledge of divine truth distinguishes this zeal as *sacred* zeal.

3. Christian zeal is devoted to good works. Having knowledge of God, whom he trusts and loves, and the duties He requires of us, the zealous Christian resolves to perform those duties, not "coldly and carelessly, as if it were no matter whether [he] performed them or no," but "heartily and zealously, with all [his] might."[28] Sacred zeal is busy and active, continually putting the Christian upon holy exploits and executions. Sin deadens the heart to all religious operations, for as the apostle said, "When I would do good, evil is present with me" (Rom. 7:21).

Lukewarmness dulls all our efforts, but zeal breathes life into all. Reynolds wrote, "It employs the mind in holy projects and designs. It sets the heart upon coveting some glorious enterprise, whereby its blessed God may be glorified. It carries head and hand to the accomplishment (as it may, or can) of its sacred aims and projections.... The zealous soul is continually saying to itself or to others, 'What shall I render to the Lord?'"[29]

---

27. William Beveridge, "The Duty of Zeal. A Sermon Preached before the Society for the Propagation of the Gospel in Foreign Parts, at the Parish Church of St. Mary-le-Bow, Feb. 21st, 1707," in *The Theological Works of William Beveridge* (Oxford: John Henry Parker, 1845), 6:453.

28. Beveridge, "The Duty of Zeal," in *Works,* 6:454.

29. Reynolds, 58–59. Cf. 1 Kings 8:18.

The zealous Christian is impatient of delay in duty. His zeal inclines him to expedition. It inflames him. When something stands in his way, he is impatient because he knows there is much to do and the time is short. He knows that delays are dangerous, opportunities are quickly lost and seldom return, the opening to take action may be shorter than he thinks, and there is no way of knowing what a day may bring forth. Thus he is loath to dismiss or put off what must be done.[30] For just as "today" is the day of salvation for those who do not believe (Ps. 95:7; Heb. 3:13; John 9:4; 12:35; Rom. 13:12), so it is the day of duty for those who do.

The zealous Christian is ready to perform whatever duty God places upon him, certainly to the utmost of his strength, even above it,[31] for he trusts the Lord to bring strength out of his weakness, and a richness of grace out of his poverty (Phil. 4:13; 2 Cor. 12:9–10). He is ready to glorify God by suffering and doing. Though the Son of Man has nowhere to lay His head (Matt. 8:19–20), the zealous Christian is glad to follow Christ wherever He goes, to the wilderness as well as to paradise, to a prison as well as to a palace.[32] He puts no limits upon his obedience other than those God Himself has set (Ex. 36:6; Deut. 4:2; 12:32) and executes his duty with all diligence and fervency (Acts 18:25).[33] He will neither drag his feet nor turn his eyes to the left or the right, but will keep himself in the way of God's commandments (Ps. 119:59). He will be "very forward to engage in them, cheerful in performing them, solicitous to do [his] utmost in them, that they may be more for quantity and better for quality than hitherto."[34] One zealous Christian, said Samuel Ward, "is worth a thousand others, one doth the work of many.... These are good factors and agents, doing God...good service...sparing no cost nor labor, and what they cannot do themselves, they do by their friends: 'Who is on my side, who?'"[35]

Knowing that the Lord has created him unto good works (Eph. 2:10) and purified him to be zealous of good works (Titus 2:14), the

---

30. Reynolds, 59.
31. Ames, 56.
32. Love, 27.
33. Ames, 56.
34. Evans, 329.
35. Ward, 79.

Christian looks more to the duty than to the reward, complaining more of his defects in performing it than the lack of expected returns. Love wrote, "Many men are content to follow God as long as there is any advantage in so doing…. So wicked men follow God till they come at a carrion, till they meet with some stinking lust, some occasion or object of sin, and then they depart from God and close with it. But David followed after God and thirsted for God even when he was 'in a dry and weary land where no water was' (Ps. 63:1)…. This is the spirit of a man who is truly zealous after the gospel."[36]

The zealous Christian will summon all the powers of soul and body to accomplish the work the Lord has given him. Bowles pressed this matter with the questions, "What should we be earnest for, if not for God and His cause? Will you be earnest for your friend, your profit, your pleasures, and cold for your God?"[37] The zealous Christian will do the Lord's work with perseverance and endurance, and, like the heavenly fire atop Mount Carmel (1 Kings 18:36–38), will burn until the work is finished.[38] If obstacles and difficulties line his way, he will not be put off; rather than abate his endeavors, these obstructions will only quicken them. As Love said, "A zealous Christian, the more you endeavor to pull him from God, he cleaves the closer to Him."[39]

4. Christian zeal begins with self-examination. Thomas Brooks said that zeal "spends itself and its greatest heat principally upon those things that concern a man's self."[40] This is particularly important in relation to the next mark of zeal—caring about others, for, as Richard Greenham said, "Never can that man be zealous to others, which never knew to be zealous to himself."[41]

He went on to explain: "True zeal casts the first stone at ourselves, and plucks the beam out of our own eyes, that we may the better draw

---

36. Love, 27–28.
37. Bowles, 24.
38. Bowles, 25.
39. Love, 28.
40. Thomas Brooks, "The Unsearchable Riches of Christ," in *The Works of Thomas Brooks* (Edinburgh: Banner of Truth, 2001), 3:55.
41. Greenham, 113.

the mote out of another's eye. And this is the condemnation of the world, that every man can pry and make a privy search into the wants of others, but they account the same wants no wants in themselves.... We call not in our consciences for those things which we dare challenge and cry out for in others."[42]

Sincere self-examination helps prevent the damnable error of hypocrisy. Greenham said of the great need for self-examination, "It has been a fearful note of hypocrites, and such as have fallen from the living God, that they have waded very deeply into others men's possessions, and gored very bloodily into the consciences of others, who never once purged their own unclean sinks at home, nor drew one drop of blood out of their own hearts."[43]

John Evans said the "first and principal province of Christian zeal is in relation to ourselves; and to other people in the second place, as we have only a secondary concern in them."[44] This means that zeal's first business is at home, where it must keep up the fervor of its own spirit in religion and in the intensity of personal obedience. If we fail in this, we are no better than hypocrites who are content to point the finger at others. "We should be warmest in concern and endeavor, that we ourselves may daily become wiser and better, that we may pull out every beam or mote out of our own eyes," Evans wrote. "And if people were thus in earnest zealous at home, a great deal of irregular zeal to others would be prevented."[45]

One way this concern manifests itself is in the sincere censure of self in both sin and liberty. The zealous Christian is more rigorous toward himself than he is to others (Matt. 7:4).[46] Greenham said, "In the truth [zeal] urges ourselves more than others, it makes us the most severe censors of our own souls, it is strictest to ourselves, and offers liberty to others; and this simplicity appears either in inward corruption or in the liberty of outward things."[47] The zealous Christian

---

42. Greenham, 114.
43. Greenham, 114.
44. Evans, 327.
45. Evans, 330.
46. Ames, 57.
47. Greenham, 114–15.

sincerely examines himself according to God's law and is most zealous against those secret infirmities which are unknown to others, but which are most grievous to him. He is familiar with his secret evils, and is so grieved by them, that he regards the sins of others as more tolerable than his own. Greenham said he learned from the sense of his own sores to deal more meekly with the sores of others.[48]

Greenham said that another attribute of true zeal is its willingness to be admonished by others just as it is careful in admonishing others.[49] How quickly do we volunteer to help others see their blind spots? And how slow are we to appreciate the brother who points out ours? But when this grace of zeal has taken hold of our hearts, we will be grateful to have others point out our sins to us, and will deal kindly, in a spirit of meekness, when faithfulness compels us to tell a brother his fault.

5. *Christian zeal cares about others.* Having caught the foxes threatening its own vineyard (Song 2:15), zeal looks away from self toward others. Evans said, "Christian zeal is not to be confined at home, to our own personal goodness; but has a still wider scope. If it is employed abroad, while our own vineyard is not kept, it is a false pretense, and justly offensive to God and man. But the due exercise of it for our own conduct being presupposed, there is a large field for its exercise still behind."[50]

The first way that true zeal reaches out to others is in desiring their salvation. Beveridge wrote, "If we have any zeal for His [God's] glory, it will appear in striving all we can to spread and propagate His said Gospel...that all nations may know Him, and serve Him, and worship Him, and give Him thanks for His great glory manifested in their redemption, and so partake of it themselves, to their eternal happiness and salvation.... And therefore all who are truly zealous for His honor, cannot but be so likewise for the salvation of all men."[51] In other words, a zealous Christian is zealous for the eternal welfare of fellow human beings.

---

48. Greenham, 115.
49. Greenham, 116.
50. Evans, 330.
51. Beveridge, "The Duty of Zeal," in *Works,* 6:455–56.

Reynolds said that sacred zeal is a lover of mankind, studious and solicitous for the truest, highest welfare for all, which can only be found in God. As a grace sent from heaven, zeal "must run the same way that divine grace does: it must be intent upon spreading the glories of grace among the inhabitants of earth; solicitous to have the intended blessings communicated and scattered about."[52] The zealous Christian would go to the house of heaven in company (Ps. 55:14), and thus is content to forego private satisfactions and advantages if it makes him more useful in bringing others to salvation. The zealous Christian hears the call of the unevangelized Macedonians saying "Come over and help us!" and eagerly heeds the call. On the other hand, zeal that is "malignant and mischievous to the true interests of mankind can never be of God," said Reynolds. Likewise, the zeal "that hates, persecutes, and murders the brethren of the human race, must needs be of hell, and from the devil, whose character is, that he was a murderer from the beginning."[53]

Second, sacred zeal earnestly desires that others live in fruitful obedience to the Lord. Zeal for the Lord not only makes us keep His commandments, but also longs to see others keep them.[54] The Lord is worthy of the devotion of all His children, who will know no better joy than in submitting to the yoke of Christ (Matt. 11:28–30).

At the center of our desire for the obedience of others is our desire that they turn from sin. We may find it extremely difficult to admonish close friends or relations to turn from sin. We would rather overlook or excuse their sins, if not absolve them altogether. Zeal is our remedy against this tendency. Greenham said, "Pure zeal is not blinded with natural affection, but it discerns and condemns sin, though it be never so nearly resident in our kindred."[55] We think we are being a true friend by accepting people as they are, warts and all. But when it comes to sin, the opposite is true. Greenham said, "He loves most naturally, that has learned to love spiritually; and he loves

---

52. Reynolds, 61.
53. Reynolds, 62.
54. Beveridge, "The Duty of Zeal," in *Works,* 6:454.
55. Greenham, 117.

most sincerely that cannot abide sin in the party loved, without some wholesome admonition."[56]

6. *Christian zeal is constant.* The zealous Christian disdains lukewarmness as much as blind fury. Nebuchadnezzar was guilty of blind fury when he heated a furnace seven times hotter than normal to consume people who would not worship him.[57] The true Christian is not hot by fits, nor starting out hot only to end up cold (Gal. 3:3). Rather, he keeps a continual tenor and temperature from beginning to end (Heb. 3:14).[58] He does not yield to faintness or despondency, for though his flesh is weak and weary, his zealous spirit is still willing and active (Mark 14:38). Reynolds said that zeal "may meet with storms, and stones, and stumbling blocks in its way; but its design and temper is to hold on, and march through all to the end."[59]

William Bates is especially helpful on this final mark of zeal. He said, "There is no counsel more directive and profitable for our arriving to an excellent degree of holiness, than this: let our progress in the way of heaven be with the same zeal, as we felt in our first entrance into it, and with the same seriousness, as when we shall come to the end of it. The first and last actions of the saints, are usually the most excellent.... But alas how often are the first heats allayed, and stronger resolutions decline to remissness."[60] When we see how cold we have become, we might heed the words of Bates: "We should with tears of confusion remember the disparity between our zealous beginnings, and slack prosecution in religion; we should blush with shame, and tremble with fear, at the strange decay of grace, and recollect ourselves, and reinforce our will to proceed with vigorous constancy."[61]

A great help toward constancy in zeal is to fix on what the Puritans called the four last things: death, judgment, heaven, and hell. Our death

---

56. Greenham, 117.
57. Ames, 57.
58. Greenham, 116.
59. Reynolds, 67.
60. William Bates, "Spiritual Perfection Unfolded and Enforced," in *The Whole Works of the Rev. William Bates* (Harrisonburg, Va.: Sprinkle Publications, 1990), 2:524–25.
61. Bates, "Spiritual Perfection," in *Works*, 2:525–26.

is imminent, our coming before the Lord in judgment is certain, and our eternal abode in either heaven or hell is inevitable. Bates urged such reflections when he said, "Let us therefore by our serious thoughts often represent to ourselves the approaches of death and judgment. This will make us contrive and contend for perfection in holiness.... Let us do those things now, which when we come to die we shall wish we had done."[62] The zealous Christian stirs his affections by lifting his thoughts to eternal matters.

The zealous Christian strives to be constant in every condition, in every duty, and against every sin.[63] He hates every sin (Mark 9:43–48) and embraces every duty (Ps. 119:6). He allows himself no sin and excuses himself from no duty. His zeal puts a constant eye on his every thought, word, and deed. He watches his thoughts with all strictness (Phil. 4:8), governs his speech with all care (Eph. 4:29; Col. 4:6), and guards his heart with all diligence (Prov. 4:23). The zealous Christian knows of no place in his life in which Christ is not Lord and considers no time in his life when the grace of zeal is unnecessary. Whatever he is given to do, he does it unto the Lord with all his might (Eccl. 9:10; Deut. 6:5; 1 Cor. 10:31).

These, then, are six major characteristics of zeal. They are the properties or marks by which zeal is distinguished. In these ways Christian zeal shows itself to be of God and for God. It is therefore not to be despised, but sought with all our might at the throne of grace. In these ways Christian zeal must run if it is true and has its source in the throne of God.

The Marks of False Religious Zeal

Some people claim to have sacred zeal and yet run in different channels than the ways of God do. The marks of their zeal show that it is of a different stock, flowing from a different spring, neither of God nor for God. When Jesus said there would be many who were false and yet professed His name, He said we would be able to tell the difference by their fruit: "Every good tree bringeth forth good fruit; but a corrupt tree

---

62. Bates, "Spiritual Perfection," in *Works*, 2:526.
63. Ames, 57.

bringeth forth evil fruit. A good tree cannot bring forth evil fruit, neither can a corrupt tree bring forth good fruit. Every tree that bringeth
not forth good fruit is hewn down, and cast into the fire. Wherefore by
their fruits ye shall know them" (Matt. 7:17–20).

Samuel Ward suggested there are many kinds of "strange fire" (Lev.
10:1–2) under the guise of true zeal, but he reduced them to three kinds:
counterfeit zeal, blind zeal, and turbulent zeal. *Counterfeit, hypocritical zeal*, he said, is the mere vigor of zeal, which looks one way while
tending another. It is the hypocritical zeal of Jehu in 2 Kings 10:16, who
boasted of eyeing the glory of the Lord, but really had his eye on his own
gain. It is the counterfeit zeal of Demetrius who cried out in praise of
Diana, but really cared only for the money that her silver idols brought
in (Acts 19:23–28). A counterfeit zeal pretends to be pursuing God's
glory while it is pursuing some private and sinister end. False zeal only
puts on the form of godliness but lacks its true power (2 Tim. 3:5).[64]

Blind or erroneous zeal, according to Romans 10:2, is not based
on knowledge. Like the spirited determination of a blind horse, it is
misplaced zeal. With this zeal, people take great pains and make great
sacrifices, yet end up falling into a pit. They are all energy, but in the
wrong direction, unto a wrong end. The apostle Paul was inflamed by
this zeal prior to meeting the Lord Jesus on the road to Damascus (Acts
22:3–4). Ward must have been thinking of Paul when he said of those
aflame with blind zeal, "Than these the devil hath no better soldiers; but
when their scales fall from their eyes, and they come into God's tents,
God hath none like unto them."[65]

The third type of zeal is *turbulent or bitter zeal*. It is referred to in
James 3:14 as bitter envying or jealousy. It is like a wildfire that sweeps
people beyond all bounds of moderation. In such people, zeal is no longer a good servant but rules as an ill master.[66] It is so different from the
heavenly fire of Christian zeal, Ward said, that a truly zealous Christian,
"whose fervency is in the spirit, not in show; in substance, not in cir-
cumstance; for God, not himself; guided by the word, not with humors;

---

64. Ward, 75.
65. Ward, 76.
66. Ward, 76.

tempered with charity, not with bitterness: such a man's worth cannot be set forth with the tongues of men and of angels."[67]

False zeal is such a grievous error threatening the church that we should strengthen this study by adding several more voices (Eccl. 4:9–10) on this matter. John Evans warned against blind zeal, saying, "Indeed heat without light, or rash and blind zeal, is the most extravagant and mischievous thing in the world; and therefore careful examination should always go before the actings of zeal. Otherwise we may be found fighting against God, when we think to do him good service; and active instruments in the devil's service through ignorance, while we flatter ourselves that we are animated by a zeal for God."[68]

The first test of zeal, then, is to determine whether it burns for a righteous cause. Evans wrote, "It should be our first care to be well assured, *that the cause is good* for which our zeal is employed, that is, that what we are zealous for, is really truth or duty; and that what we are zealous against, is certainly false or evil."[69]

The importance of whether we are zealous "in a good thing" (Gal. 4:18) needs to be pressed upon our conscience because danger exists on both sides of the narrow path of true zeal. A person can be falsely zealous in a true thing or truly zealous in a false thing. Thomas Adams said, "Some have a true zeal of a false religion, and some have a false zeal of a true religion. Paul, prior to his conversion, had a true zeal of a false religion [Gal. 1:14].... The Laodiceans had a false, or rather no zeal, of a true religion [Rev. 3:15]."[70]

Oliver Bowles warned believers to be diligent to determine that our zeal is of the right stamp since "as every [other] grace so zeal may and often does have its counterfeit."[71] Therefore it is vital that we know what we are zealous about. The crowd that gathered in Acts 19:28–34, cried out for two hours, "Great is Diana of the Ephesians" (v. 34). Yet, the text specifically says that most of them "knew not wherefore they were

---

67. Ward, 77.

68. Evans, 324.

69. Evans, 323.

70. Thomas Adams, "Heaven Made Sure; or, The Certainty of Salvation," in *The Works of Thomas Adams* (Edinburgh: James Nichol, 1861), 1:63.

71. Bowles, 27.

come together" (v. 32). Evans warned of such blindness in our zeal: "To be zealous for we know not what, is as bad as to *worship we know not what*."[72] He continued:

> And howsoever positive and confident we may be, after all our warmth, we may be on the wrong side, if our assurance be not the result of a sincere and impartial inquiry. And indeed, if we should happen to be in the right, yet a blind and random zeal, even for truth itself, cannot be acceptable to God; because it is rather by chance, than upon reasonable evidence, that our zeal is on the right side. Every man therefore is bound, before he gives a loose to his zeal, to use the best helps in his power for discovering the mind of God; and no man should suffer his zeal to outrun his knowledge, or to exceed the evidence he has of the truth or falsehood, of the good or evil of these things.[73]

The great danger of false zeal cannot be overestimated. John Flavel, in his *Treatise of the Soul of Man*, described a blind and false zeal about externals as "a way of ruining precious souls," and "a way to hell," which he defined as "the way of formal hypocrisy in religion, and zeal about the externals of worship."[74] He added, "Nothing is more common, than to find men hot and zealous against false worship, whilst their hearts are as cold as a stone in the *vitals*, and *essentials* of *true religion*."[75] Flavel said the Pharisees were guilty of false zeal in being overly zealous for man-made traditions and the external ceremonies of the law (Matt. 15:7–9), while inwardly they were "full of all filthiness."

Under the impulse of false zeal, Flavel said, "Religion runs into stalk, and blade, into leaves, and suckers, which should be concocted into pith and fruit; yea, it is of sad consideration, that amongst many high pretenders to reformation, their zeal, which should nourish the vitals of religion, and maintain their daily work of mortification and communion with God, spends itself in some by-opinion, whilst practical godliness visibly languisheth in their conversations."[76] Those with false zeal hate doctrinal errors but perish by practical ones. They hate

---

72. Cf. John 4:22a.
73. Evans, 324–25.
74. John Flavel, "A Treatise of the Soul of Man," in *The Works of John Flavel* (Edinburgh: Banner of Truth, 1968), 3:214.
75. Flavel, "The Soul of Man," in *Works,* 3:216.
76. Flavel, "The Soul of Man," in *Works,* 3:215.

false doctrine but perish by a false heart.[77] George Swinnock added this lament against false zeal, "Oh devout ungodliness, or ungodly devotion! How few take such pains to go to heaven, as many do to go to hell…. Alas! what sorrow does this call for and command! that men should be so hot and fiery in will-worship, in false worship."[78]

Fiery zeal in a wrong cause is indeed lamentable, but what must be said of coldness or lukewarmness in the Christian life? Christopher Love said that covetous men are said to "pant after the dust of the earth" (Amos 2:7). They are so eager in their pursuit of the world that they run themselves out of breath (Ps. 59:6). In comparison, "toward the things of eternity we are as if we were all Stoics and had no passions in us. As hot as fire for earth and as cold as any ice for heaven. Oh, how many pant after the earth who have no breathing after heaven!"[79]

Swinnock's comments on the zeal and passion with which wicked people pursue superstition deserve to be quoted at length. We should lay them before the Lord with much prayer that God would see, hear, and act upon our cry for Christian zeal to fill us once again. Comparing the lukewarm Christian to the men of this world, Swinnock said,

> silly man hangs off from his Maker—[so] that neither entreaties, nor threatenings, nor the word, nor the works of God, nor hope of heaven, nor fear of hell, can quicken or hasten him to his happiness. Who would imagine that a reasonable soul should act so much against sense and reason? Where is that saint that is not shamed by the very damned? Sinners drive furiously, like Jehu, against their God, their sovereign; but saints, like Egyptians, drive heavily, though they are marching in the road to the heavenly Canaan. Ah, who presseth towards the mark for the prize of high calling? Who works so hard to be preferred to the beatific vision, as wicked men do to be punished with eternal destruction? They sweat at sowing in the devil's field, when all they shall reap thereby will be damnation, and thou freezest in seeking God's favor, when the fruit thereof will be everlasting salvation.[80]

---

77. Flavel, "The Soul of Man," in *Works,* 3:215.
78. George Swinnock, "The Christian Man's Calling," in *The Works of George Swinnock* (Edinburgh: Banner of Truth, 1992), 1:74–75.
79. Love, 15.
80. Swinnock, "Christian Man's Calling," in *Works,* 1:78–79.

"Consider and mourn," Swinnock continued, "that the deceitful world, that superstition, that the loathsome monster sin, should have so many and such eager, earnest suitors; and yet godliness should be by most wholly slighted, and at best but coldly courted! Surely this ought to be for a lamentation."[81]

Thomas Brooks warned against the false zeal that threatens weak Christians by outstripping their wisdom and knowledge. The disciples were guilty of such false zeal in Luke 9:54 when they wanted to call fire from heaven to consume the unwelcoming Samaritans. Brooks said, "But mark what Christ says [v. 55]: 'Ye know not what manner of spirits ye are of'; that is, ye know not what spirit acts you. You think that you are acted by such a spirit as Elijah of old was acted by, but you err, says Christ; 'you have a zeal, but not according to knowledge,' therefore it is a human affection and not a divine motion."[82]

The apostle Paul said it is good to be zealous ("zealously affected") in a good thing (Gal. 4:18), but zeal that is not united to knowledge is profitable to no one. "Zeal is like a fire: in the chimney it is one of the best servants, but out of the chimney it is one of the worst masters," said Brooks. "Zeal kept by knowledge and wisdom, in its proper place, is a choice servant to Christ and saints; but zeal not bounded by wisdom and knowledge, is the high way to undo all, and to make a hell for many at once."[83]

How, then, may false zeal be known? Christopher Love offered the following marks that distinguish false zeal from true Christian zeal.[84] To his comments we will add a few remarks given by Oliver Bowles in his sermon before the Westminster Assembly.

1. The difference is most obvious in trivial and circumstantial matters. The Pharisees were overzealous about washing their vessels and their hands before eating, but they failed to be observant about the washing or cleansing of their heart. "They were very violent for the linen ephod,

---

81. Swinnock, "Christian Man's Calling," in *Works,* 1:79.
82. Brooks, "The Unsearchable Riches of Christ," in *Works*, 3:54.
83. Brooks, "The Unsearchable Riches of Christ," in *Works*, 3:54–55.
84. Love, 29–33.

though it may be there was a leprous skin under it," Love said.[85] By contrast, a godly man is most concerned with those things that most glorify God and save his soul.

2. *False zeal is kindled by passion and vainglory* in correcting others, whereas true zeal is kindled by holy indignation against sin, and a loving concern for the sinner.

3. *False zeal leads a person beyond the bounds of his place and calling.* Such was the violence of Saul (1 Sam. 13:13) and of Peter (Mark 8:32). By contrast, holy violence keeps a person zealous in his place, respectful towards his superiors, and tender towards his inferiors whom he must admonish. "Fire in its place is good and useful, but out of its place how hurtful and destructive it is," Love said.[86]

4. *False zeal is more eager at first than at the end.* But a holy zeal receives the commendation of Thyatira that her last works were more than her first (Rev. 2:19). Bowles explained: "We have many that begin well, are hot and eager while in such a company, while they have such props, while carried on by such hopes, while not assaulted with such temptations, while they thought the cause would go thus they were hot and eager in the work of reformation, but as things alter from without, they alter from within, even to the total remitting of their zeal."[87]

5. *False zeal is discouraged by the difficulties of religion* (Matt. 8:19–20). In contrast, holy zeal is quickened by opposition and persecution. Bowles said that if the zeal is true, "as that which has the cause of God in the eye, then tract of time, multitude of discouragements, falseness of men deserting the cause, strength of oppositions will not tire out a man's spirit. Zeal makes men resolute, difficulties are but whetstones to their fortitude, it steels men's spirits with an undaunted magnanimity."[88]

---

85. Love, 29.
86. Love, 30.
87. Bowles, 28–29.
88. Bowles, 29.

6. False zeal is led more by example than by rule. It is the mindless violence of the crowd who shouted for Diana of Ephesus (Acts 19:32), whereas Christian zeal is led by Scripture as a rule (Isa. 8:20).

7. A person with false zeal is busy with controversies and circumstances in religion. With this type of false zeal, Saul violently objected to eating the blood of sacrifices (1 Sam. 14:32–33) but made no scruple against shedding the blood of the priests of Nob (1 Sam. 22:19). True zeal makes a person conversant in the practical things of Christianity (Titus 2:14).

8. False zeal is uneven; there is no uniformity to it. It is violent against some sins, but not all. It is for some duties, but not all. It is eager to exercise some graces, but not all (2 Kings 10:28, 31). Holy zeal, by contrast, is uniform. It makes a truly zealous person lash out against every sin. It makes a person walk in all of God's commandments (Ps. 119:6). Bowles said, "If zeal be right, she will not hate ought of what lies under the command of God…. It's false zeal that…makes nothing of small matters; true zeal drives on the work of reformation so as it leaves not the least remnants of Baal, removes all the high places."[89]

9. Blind zeal makes a person disruptive of human societies and civil governments. It makes him despise and refute authority. But holy zeal is quiet and peaceable towards men. Though a truly zealous person pursues heaven with violence, yet while on this earth he desires to "lead a quiet and peaceable life, in all godliness and honesty" (1 Tim. 2:2).

10. False zeal proceeds from natural rashness. It is marked by stoutness of heart towards both God and man. But Christian zeal is marked by self-humiliation before the Lord (Rev. 3:19). Zeal for God must be joined with the breaking of our own hearts (2 Cor. 7:11).

---

89. Bowles, 28.

Conclusion

Can zeal be praised, urged, or impressed too much upon the consciences of today's Christians? We are convinced that the answer is no. We must be zealous in that one true faith by which God has made Himself known to sinful man (John 14:6) and through which reconciliation with the thrice holy God is given to us (2 Cor. 5:18–21). Should we not burn as hot for God and His kingdom as the fire of zeal will enable us? Does the Lord call us to anything less than zeal in Christianity? Is there any ground in Scripture to assume that a Christian life of mediocrity and coldness will give us confidence in the Judgment Day?

What Christian will be ashamed of having been overly zealous on the Day of Judgment, or think he gave up too much for Christ when he beholds His beloved face? As William Jenkyn said, "There may be a sinful, damnable moderation. Following Christ afar off in this world is no sign that we shall be near Him in the next."[90] We commend this sacred zeal to you as the heavenly and fiery grace by which saints both past and present must take the kingdom of heaven (Matt. 11:12).

Study Questions

1. Read John 2:13–17. Based on Christ's example, how would you define zeal for God?

2. Zeal is compared to a fire in the soul, sometimes translated "fervent" or "burning" (Acts 18:25; Rom. 12:11). How is zeal like an inward flame? How does zeal inflame the rest of our lives?

3. Read Psalm 119:136, 139. How does a zealous love for God lead us to react to sin? When was the last time you grieved deeply over the sins of those around you?

---

90. William Jenkyn, *An Exposition upon the Epistle of Jude* (Minneapolis: James & Klock, 1976), 104.

4. Read Romans 10:2. What fault did Paul find with the zeal of many of his Hebrew kinsmen? Why must Scripture control zeal?

5. Read Matthew 7:3–5. What is the difference between true zeal and hypocritical zeal? How will true zeal move us to respond when someone corrects us for our sins?

6. Read Colossians 4:12–13. Epaphras had "great zeal for you." What did he desire for them? How did he seek to get it? How should zeal for the Lord move us to serve others?

7. John Evans said, "Indeed heat without light, or rash and blind zeal, is the most extravagant and mischievous thing in the world." Give some examples you have seen or heard of false zeal. How has it been destructive to God's glory and man's good?

8. List some key differences between true zeal for God and false zeal. How can we discern in ourselves whether our zeal is good or evil?

9. Read Galatians 1:13–14. What was Paul zealous for before his conversion? What did that move him to do? What does that teach us about false zeal?

10. What is one thing that you could take from this chapter and start to pray for God to work in your life? What Scripture text could you use to encourage and direct these prayers?

The Necessity and Motives
of Christian Zeal

In chapter 1, we established a working definition of Christian zeal, identified many of its characteristics or marks, and exposed the signs of false zeal. Now we are ready to discuss the necessity of zeal and suggest several reasons why Christians must seek zeal from the Lord.

The Necessity of Christian Zeal

Zeal is a gift of God and cannot be acquired by mere human effort, but God has established the means by which we can attain it. If that were not so, He would not have charged the Laodiceans to be zealous (Rev. 3:19).[1]

Many things make sacred zeal a necessary grace. First of all, zeal is necessary because of its very nature. In the last chapter we learned that zeal "must be the companion of every grace";[2] is "a qualification which should attend us in the exercise of grace, and in the performance of every duty";[3] and "heats a man's work with a holy fervor; which are, without that, a cold sacrifice to God."[4] Can we possibly get along in religion—which is nothing less than duty inflamed and enabled by grace—without zeal?

Thomas Adams asserted a Christian cannot live without zeal. He wrote, "A soul without zeal doth as hardly live as a body without a

---

1. These means will be addressed more specifically in chapter 6.
2. Annesley, "How May We Attain?" in *Puritan Sermons,* 1:616.
3. Evans, 320.
4. Adams, "Heaven Made Sure," in *Works,* 1:374–75.

liver[5]...[so] we may say of zeal, it is the very cistern whence all other graces issue forth into our lives.... In the soul, other graces, as faith, hope, charity, repentance, did first rather breed zeal; but zeal being once enkindled, doth minister nutrimental heat to all these, and is indeed the best sacrifice that we can offer to God. Without zeal, all are like the oblation [offering] of Cain."[6]

Second, zeal is necessary because God commands it.[7] Is not the goal of the first four commandments that we should worship the Lord with zeal?[8] We are to pledge allegiance to no other gods but the living God; to worship Him with strict diligence and devotion to His commands for worship; to honor and revere His name and all the means by which He reveals Himself to us; and to forego all worldly things to honor and sanctify His Day. How can these commands require anything less than holy zeal?

Then, too, Ecclesiastes 9:10 commands us, "Whatsoever thy hand findeth to do, do it with thy might." The New Testament counterpart to that is Romans 12:11, which tells us to be "not slothful in business," but "fervent in spirit."[9] These verses tell us there is much work that still needs to be done; much work to which the Lord calls us and for which we will one day give an account.

But we will also give an account of *how* we have done that work. If we have not done it with all our might, we have not done it aright; if we have done it with cold affections, we have not done it aright. Our duties are to be done with fervency of spirit both for the work itself and for God who called us to it. Swinnock said, "When we deal with our equals, with them that stand upon the same level with us, we may deal as men...[but] in things that appertain to God, we must give double weight, double measure, double care, double diligence; though men be slothful and sluggish in the service of men, yet they must be fiery and 'fervent in spirit' when they are 'serving the Lord' (Rom. 12:11)."[10]

---

5. In ancient and medieval medicine, the liver was regarded as the *fons sanguinis*, the source of blood, and therefore the seat of the life of the body.

6. Adams, "Heaven Made Sure," in *Works*, 1.375.

7. Love, 22.

8. Greenham, 113.

9. Literally, "in the Spirit being hot."

10. Swinnock, "The Christian Man's Calling," in *Works*, 1:55–56.

Third, zeal is necessary because of the very nature of religion.[11] Religion is important, Evans said, because it is "that wherein the honor of God, the present welfare of the world, and the everlasting interest of ourselves and others is more concerned than in anything else."[12] The aims and essentials of true religion deserve and demand fervency, ardor, and zeal. To dispense with zeal in religion is to hold to its form while denying its power (2 Tim. 3:5).

Many difficulties in personal religion certainly indicate the need for Christian zeal. Evans wrote, "There are many indispositions within ourselves, and many oppositions from without, that will never be surmounted without a holy fervor.... Indeed the maintenance of a right zeal is of the utmost consequence for our own security against infection by the many evils around us."[13]

Consider, for example, the sincerity that religion demands. Can we claim to love God and yet not be zealous *for* Him and *against* evil? Evans said, "If we love God, we shall hate evil.... And so great is his excellence, and sin's evil, that if our affections be right set between both, we cannot remain cold and indifferent for the one against the other."[14] Without zeal our Christianity is lifeless and cold. It is no more real than show and no warmer than a painted image of a fire.

Also consider that divine acceptance cannot be obtained without zeal.[15] Christ plainly declares this in Revelation 3:19 when He threatens the Laodicean church with utter rejection ("I will spue thee out of my mouth") because her members are neither cold nor hot. Evans asserts, "He therefore calls them to repentance, and to resume a warmth and spirit in religion, as ever they would avoid so dreadful a doom."[16]

Fourth, zeal is necessary because of our past and present estate.[17] Remember how zealous we were in the ways of sin in the past, how violently we sought pleasure in evil ways, and how headstrong we were

---

11. Evans, 335–37.
12. Evans, 335.
13. Evans, 335–36.
14. Evans, 336.
15. Evans, 336.
16. Evans, 336.
17. Love, 23.

in the pursuit of sin? Yet the apostle Paul tells us in Romans 6:19 that we are to give ourselves to holiness as (in the same manner) we once gave ourselves to sin. We are to be as devoted to God now as we were formerly devoted to ourselves; and as given over to righteousness now as we were formerly given to wickedness. We must give ourselves as freely and wholly to Christian duty now as we formerly gave ourselves to the pleasures of sin. How can we do what God requires without being inflamed with zeal for the paths of righteousness and God's law, that is equal to or greater than our former zeal for sin?

Consider too the temptations we must battle against as believers. How can we resist evil if our new affection for holiness is not equally strong as our old affection for evil? It is obvious that lukewarm affection for God will be unable to overcome the mighty temptations that beset us. The zealous use of the means of grace is a great help for withstanding such temptation.

Fifth, zeal is necessary because of our enemy. First Peter 5:8 says, "Be sober, be vigilant; because your adversary the devil, as a roaring lion, walketh about, seeking whom he may devour." Christopher Love pressed the need for vigilance against Satan, saying, "He is said to be an adversary. Now an adversary will watch all opportunities for your hurt, and will intently set upon it." He is a lion, not a lamb. A lion is a savage, fierce, and furious creature. He is not asleep but roaring. He is not standing still, content with the prey he already has, but roaming for more. Though Satan has sought to devour souls ever since Adam's fall, he goes about looking for more. He labors to fill hell with souls. He seeks those whom he may devour. "The devil watches," Love said, "and do you sleep?"[18]

How can we oppose such an enemy unless we are awake and ablaze with Christian zeal? The enemy stalks us and watches our every move, zealous in his ravenous hunger for our destruction. Christian zeal is as necessary as vigilance to oppose such a foe.

Sixth, zeal is necessary because of the present condition of mankind.[19] How violent the wicked are against truth! Must we not be as

---

18. Love, 23–24.
19. Love, 24.

eager in the profession of truth as the wicked are in opposing it? Christopher Love wrote, "Wicked men are as swift as dromedaries in the ways of sin, and will you be as a dull ass in the service of God? Shall a man run fast in a way of sin to destroy his soul, and will you but creep in the ways of God to save your soul? Shall wicked men run fast to hell, and will you but creep slowly to heaven? Shall a man make speed to the place of execution, and will you but move slowly towards a crown and throne? Shall wicked men not be ashamed to show their rage in a sinful course, and shall godly men be ashamed to be zealous in the ways of God?"[20] They weary themselves to commit iniquity, and will you not do as much for God as they do for Satan?[21]

Consider how zealous the saints of old were for God. Caleb and Joshua followed God fully (Num. 14:24), while their hypocritical comrades followed God by halts and halves. David gave himself no rest until he found a place for God's house (Ps. 132:4–5). Daniel knew that he would be cast into the den of lions for praying to his God, yet he did not cease to pray three times a day (Dan. 6:10). And who were the persons described in Hebrews 11:38 as those "of whom the world was not worthy," but men and women of zeal? These zealous saints were given to us as examples, so that we, being "compassed about with so great a cloud of witnesses" (Heb. 12:1), might ourselves be zealous for the Lord. Given the condition of evil men who oppose the truth, and of good men who have been zealous for the truth, Christian zeal is a necessary grace.

Finally, zeal is necessary in our quest for salvation and the kingdom of God.[22] Luke 13:23 tells us that a question was put to Jesus: "Lord, are there few that be saved?" He responds, "Strive to enter in at the strait gate: for many, I say unto you, will seek to enter in, and shall not be able." We are to contend or strive[23] for heaven just as an athlete strives for victory. It is not enough merely to seek for the gate, for many seekers shall never find it. "The gate leading to life is strait, and only those who strive with might and main, and whole-heartedly to enter, will be

---

20. Love, 24. Cf. Jer. 8:6; 9:5.
21. Love, 24.
22. Love, 25.
23. Greek: *agonizomai,* to contend for a prize.

saved," writes Norval Geldenhuys;[24] or as Christopher Love said, we must strive for heaven with "a kind of holy impatience."[25]

We cannot expect to get to heaven walking at a leisurely pace. Zealous running, as in a race, is required to obtain the crown (1 Cor. 9:24–25). Love wrote, "Heaven is compared to a hill and hell to a pit. It will cost a man sweat and labor to get up a hill, but it is an easy thing to go down into a pit. Heaven is as Canaan…though a land of promise, yet of conquest too…[so] heaven is not had without eagerness. Luke 16:16 says, 'Every man presseth into it.' It is an allusion to soldiers who storm a city or strong garrison with all the speed and violence they can. Should soldiers go about that great work in a marching pace, they might all be cut off."[26]

Can anyone get to heaven without zeal? Love wrote, "Take heed you do not think you shall ever go to heaven without this holy zeal and violence.… You can never get to heaven unless you strive to enter in at the strait gate. You must strive till you sweat. You must strive with all your might, and all will be little enough. Take heed, therefore, you do not think it an easy thing to go to heaven. But withal take this: though you cannot go to heaven *without* this holy violence, you shall never go to heaven *for* it."[27]

We must be zealous for God. To be sure, we will not gain entrance into heaven or merit acceptance from God by mere human striving or fervency; but we, who are heirs of heaven and co-heirs with Christ by grace (Rom. 8:15–17), who are accepted by God in union with Christ (Eph. 1:6) by God's electing grace (Eph. 1:4), will not get to heaven without Christian zeal. It is not something that may or may not be had, but is the Godward fervency of Spirit that is the principal mark of a Christian. Without it, we are cold or lukewarm, neither of which God will own (Rev. 3:15–19).

Given the necessity of zeal, let us consider the motives that compel us to ask God for holy zeal that will set us ablaze with such heavenly fervor

---

24. Norval Geldenhuys, *Commentary on the Gospel of Luke* (Grand Rapids: Eerdmans, 1951), 380.

25. Love, 25.

26. Love, 25–26.

27. Love, 36. Cf. James 1:25.

that we may labor mightily for Him and His cause. For if zeal is a necessary grace, then to whom can we go for it, if not to the God of all grace? Has not He, who has called us unto His eternal glory by Christ Jesus, promised that He will make us perfect, "stablish, strengthen, and settle" us (1 Pet. 5:10)? Shall not such perfection include the gift of zeal?

The Motives for Christian Zeal

Discussion of the motives for zeal will naturally overlap with the necessity for zeal since what makes zeal necessary should motivate us to acquire it. If we saw no need for zeal, there would be no motivation to strive for it. The greater the need for something, the greater the motive. Therefore, any overlap of this section with the former one is in no way superfluous. It is necessary that we have both the need for zeal and the obligation to pursue zeal pressed upon our consciences. Therefore, let us consider some motivations to ask God for Christian zeal in proportion to our great need.

1. We should be motivated by Christ's purchase. Titus 2:14 says Christ "gave himself for us, that he might redeem us from all iniquity, and purify unto himself a peculiar people, zealous of good works." There was a double purpose for Christ's death, namely, that we might, first, be redeemed from sin in all its forms, and second, be ardent in obeying God's voice and keeping His covenant (cf. Exodus 19:5). Christ purchased us in order to set us free from bondage to sin, and to lead us into the greater freedom of serving our God, "whose service is perfect freedom."[28]

From this text it is clear that Christ's redemption or purchase was not an end in itself. The manner of the purchase, and the price that was paid, was intended to leave its mark on those for whom He died, that they should be "zealous for good works." Are you zealous for good works? You have been "created in Christ Jesus unto good works, which God hath before ordained [or prepared] that we should walk in them" (Eph. 2:10). They are a path for your feet; are you zealously walking in

---

28. "Collect for Peace," Order for Morning Prayer, *Book of Common Prayer* (1662).

them? Thomas Manton said, "As in a tree, the sap and life is hid, but the fruit and apples do appear, so zeal of good works is that which appears, and so it manifests and clears up your condition."[29] Has zeal so "cleared up your condition" that it manifests to your conscience and to others that you are the Lord's?

Christ came to redeem you from all iniquity, including the iniquity of spiritual coldness and lukewarmness. He redeemed you *unto* *zeal*.[30] Manton wrote, "They that live at a low rate of holiness cross and disgrace the whole design of the gospel."[31] How then do you live? Has Christ come all this way and stooped so low and suffered so much for nothing? Can you report to the Master that you have doubled the talents that He gave you, or will you have to admit that you buried yours (Matt. 25:19–29)? If you admit that you lack the zeal the apostle speaks of, what excuse can you offer?

You cannot say that Christ does not want you to be zealous, or that He meant it for elite Christians, but not for "average" Christians like you. You cannot say that you wanted to be zealous, and would have been, if Christ had purchased it. Nor can you say you were under no obligation to be zealous, or that your "moderate zeal" does not fall short of your duty and calling. You are without excuse. You have been purchased for zeal by the Mediator's precious blood. Reynolds wrote, "As the great redemption deserves and claims your highest zeal for the zealous Author of it, so you demonstrate yourselves unworthy of it, you sacrilegiously defeat the end of it, as long as your hearts are destitute of sacred zeal. Has the Mediator purchased a peculiar people to Himself, how unfit will they be for Him? How unlike to Him? How unmeet to be near Him, to minister to Him, or stand about His throne, as long as they are cold in love and distant from deserved zeal?"[32]

Do you expect a just return upon your earthly investments, a just recompense for your earthly labors, a just recognition for your

---

29. Thomas Manton, Sermon XXII, "Zealous of Good Works," from "Sermons upon Titus ii. 11–14," in *The Complete Works of Thomas Manton* (London: James Nisbet, 1874), 16:281.

30. Reynolds, 198.

31. Manton, "Zealous of Good Works," in *Works,* 16:282.

32. Reynolds, 198.

workmanship? These cost you only sweat and hard work, while Christ's investment in your salvation, His labors to secure your holiness, His work to purchase your zeal, cost Him His body and blood. How much more must He expect you to be zealous for Him?

2. We should be motivated by the example of our Lord.[33] Christ was so zealous in obedience that some people who professed His name took offense that He behaved so much like a servant. Again and again we read in John's Gospel that Christ did everything for His Father's glory. He did not seek His own will but the will of the Father who sent Him (John 5:30). His teaching was not His own, but "his that sent me" (John 7:16). He insisted that even His works were not His own, but the works of "him that sent me" (John 9:4). They were the works of the Father done through Him (John 14:10). He said, "The Son can do nothing of himself, but what he seeth the Father do" (John 5:10).

The Son was so zealous for the Father's will and glory, so perfectly walking the path prepared beforehand for His feet, and so perfectly declaring the Father's doctrine, that He could say, "I do always those things that please him" (John 8:29). With such a Son, it is no wonder that the work of God is "that ye believe on him whom he hath sent" (John 6:29). It is no wonder that everyone who comes to Christ in faith is drawn by the Father (John 6:44), who takes delight in so zealous a Son.

Zeal for His Father so consumed Jesus (John 2:17) that He took every opportunity in public, in private, on a boat, in the fields, in the streets, at the supper table, in the midst of Jerusalem, or on His way through Samaria, to proclaim the salvation that He came to accomplish for His Father. Because He was set apart for this work (Ps. 40:6–10; Mark 1:9–11), He did not mingle in secular affairs but devoted Himself entirely to the work that His Father gave Him, for He knew the hour of darkness would soon be upon Him (John 9:4; Acts 10:38).

Jesus preached often and even spent nights in prayer. He took every opportunity to teach His disciples the mysteries of the kingdom, which were hidden from the crowds who followed Him for

---

33. Reynolds, 195.

their belly's sake (John 6:26–27). His zeal for the Father's glory continued unabated through all opposition and suffering. Indeed, His zeal burned hotter toward the end when death was closing in upon Him. That zeal showed itself in such words as, "But that the world may know that I love the Father; and as the Father gave me commandment, even so I do. Arise, let us go hence" (John 14:31). When Peter attempted to rescue his Master by force, Jesus said, "Put up thy sword into the sheath: the cup which my Father hath given me, shall I not drink it?" (John 18:11).

This is to not to say that Christ never rested. He urged His disciples to come apart "and rest awhile" (Mark 6:31), and took the opportunity to do likewise when He could. Christ was no ascetic; He obeyed the sixth commandment which requires a sober use of meat, drink, rest, sleep, and work (cf. Westminster Larger Catechism, Q. 135). Zeal for obedience also means zealous stewardship of our physical resources.

May not this Savior look to you who follow Him, who profess His name, whom He has redeemed with His blood and sealed with His Spirit, to whom He has given the benefit of His example, and who have His mind, expecting you to be zealous, even as He was? Reynolds said, "Justly may He command His servants, a sacred, importunate zeal, since He Himself hath been such a pattern and example of it."[34]

Peter said that Christ left us that example so that we might walk in His steps (1 Pet. 2:21). He purchased your redemption by holiness wrought in the flesh. He lived out for you the very holiness which He purchased for you, and now promises to work in you. He now calls you to that walk in the same zeal that marked His every word and deed. He calls you to deny yourself as He did, to take up the cross as He did, to devote yourself to the will of God as He did, to work while it is day as He did, and to press on in the way until the work is finished as He did. Where then is your zeal?

Christ was aflame with love for souls, aflame with hatred for sin, aflame with compassion for the hurting, aflame with grief for the obstinate, aflame with love for His sheep, and aflame with delight for the

---

34. Reynolds, 196.

Father's will. Where then is your zeal? Consider your relation to the triune God. Is the name of Him who was consumed by zeal (John 2:17) upon you? Is the Spirit of Him who was so zealous for the Father's will that He set His face to do it with unwavering determination (Luke 9:51) within you? Is the Father of Him for whose house He was consumed with zeal (John 2:17) your Father? Why then are you not zealous?

3. We should be motivated by people who are violent in the ways of sin, lest they serve Satan better than we serve God.[35] People of this world are industrious, vigorous, and resolute in the ways of sin, while we are negligent, cold, and inconstant in the service of righteousness. They disregard all reproofs and counsel; they grieve friends and relatives who stand in their way; they readily venture into great dangers; they waste their wealth, macerate their bodies, and in the end die as martyrs to lust and sin. They are zealous in following the way to hell, while many of us are sluggish on the path to heaven. They break body and bone for hell while we are loath to break flesh and skin for glory.[36]

Consider for a moment the description of a horse riding into battle in Job 39:19–25. The horse mocks fear and does not turn away from a threatening sword. Rather, it rejoices at the sound of the trumpet that signals the beginning of war. The horse smells the battle in the distance and perks up its ears at the shouting of captains. It is aflame with such a passion to rush into battle that nothing can deter it from its course. Though it may lose its life, it rages fearless into the battle.

The wicked are like that animal, says the Lord, for "no man repented him of his wickedness, saying, What have I done? Every one turned to his course, as the horse rusheth into the battle" (Jer. 8:6). Their heart is so set on evil (Eccl. 8:11) that they weary themselves to commit iniquity (Jer. 9:5; Hab. 2:13) and cannot sleep until they have done it (Prov. 4:16). Manton wrote, "How active are wicked men for the kingdom of darkness! How zealous and earnest to ruin themselves, as if they could not be damned soon enough!"[37]

---

35. Manton, "Zealous of Good Works," in *Works,* 16:284.
36. Reynolds, 218–20.
37. Manton, "Zealous of Good Works," in *Works,* 16:284.

They rush forth without the least consideration that what they are doing will cost them eternal life and their business will bring them into spiritual bankruptcy. They rush forth and "draw iniquity with cords of vanity, and sin as it were with a cart rope" (Isa. 5:18). In other words, "they would sin though it cost them a great deal of pains and sorrow, and though they could not sin at a cheap rate…it is horrid work, yet they delight in it, toiling and tiring themselves as beasts at a plough."[38]

Does this not provoke you, believer, to be zealous for God? "Oh! How can you look upon such a spectacle as this without shame, that a lust should have more power with them than the love of God with you?"[39] Will you stand idly by and let them take more pains to undo their souls than you do to save yours?

Can you watch them sweat and pant as they drag their sin behind them or exhaust themselves by pushing their sin before them, denying whatever it costs without being provoked by it? Do you do that much for God? Do sinners rush into wickedness faster than you rush into duty? Do they suffer more pain and pay a greater price for what they want than you are willing to do for God? They work for a hard master, earning bitter wages here and everlasting damnation hereafter, yet they will not be put off their course. But you labor for a tender Master whose yoke is easy, giving you joy and peace here, and everlasting pleasures hereafter. Where then is your zeal?

4. We should be motivated by the passing of time.[40] Some of us may have come to the Lord after many years of pursuing the lusts of the world. Many years "must be penned down as good for nothing, or worse than nothing; consumed in the way to death and destruction."[41] Others of us may have served the Lord for many years, but with slovenly work at the pace of a snail. Consider how much time has been wasted (1 Pet. 4:3).

How urgent it is, then, to redeem the time that is still before us (Eph. 5:17). Do we expect the Lord to be pleased with our laziness?

---

38. Manton, "Zealous of Good Works," in *Works,* 16:284
39. Manton, "Zealous of Good Works," in *Works,* 16:285.
40. Manton, "Zealous of Good Works," in *Works,* 16:286.
41. Reynolds, 224.

Do we expect Him not to care if we fold our hands and slumber (Prov. 6:10)? How can we continue to waste time when so much has already passed? We have wasted the vigor of our youth in sin, ease, and laziness. We have little left for the Lord but the dregs of old age. These dregs may yet live, but only if breathed on and stoked into life by zeal.

It may be that you have wasted your youth and can see that life's day is far spent, and the night is at hand. Yes, the day is *nearly* spent, but it is yet to *be* spent. So rise! Gird up your loins and run the race set before you! The battle still rages, the warriors still cry. With the might of the horse and the swiftness of the deer, make haste to join the ranks; press forward to the front lines, and fight with those who are so consumed with zeal for the Lord of hosts that they speak neither of age nor of remaining time, but give themselves to the battle as if they had their full might! Now is the time when you should mend your pace, double your diligence, and be zealous for the Lord your God.[42]

5. We should be motivated by the enemy of our faith who is so violent against us.[43] How zealous is the devil in his rage against us, not only prowling around like a lion with every intent to devour us (1 Pet. 5:8), but also lurking near us in all that we do. He stalks us to our workplaces, playing places, eating places, praying places, and worship places. He waits for us, to turn our heads, lower our defenses, and fall asleep, and then he strikes us with all the force at his command. Manton said, "Birds are seldom taken in their flight, but when they rest and pitch; so Satan has no advantage against us when we are upon our course and wing, when we make speed to heaven, and are zealous and earnest in our flight."[44] As sure as we begin cooling in our affections, Satan will strike in subtle ways—even by coddling us to death. Christopher Love asked, "Shall we not be as violent to save our souls as the devil is to damn them?"[45]

Where then is your zeal? Can you pause, knowing that Satan is ready to torch the staff upon which you lean? Can you draw back

---

42. Manton, "Zealous of Good Works," in *Works,* 16:287.
43. Manton, "Zealous of Good Works," in *Works,* 16:287.
44. Manton, "Zealous of Good Works," in *Works,* 16:287–88.
45. Love, 23.

from the battle when the enemy's every breath rages with the might of a host of evil? Can you quit throwing water upon the fire of your sin when Satan himself has charge of the bellows? He who rages against you cannot be underestimated. He is but a creature, yes, but the place from which he fell was higher than the place where you now stand. And in the providence and wisdom of God, this monster has retained many of his natural advantages, which makes him older, stronger, more enduring, more patient, and more zealous than you are. What will you do without Christian zeal? Do you dare to face him in your natural strength? You will be sorely defeated. His zeal is set on fire by hell and can only be quenched by the heavenly fire of God-given sacred zeal, which is grounded in our great Savior and Lord.

Thanks be to God that our Savior is stronger than the devil, for He is Lord whereas the devil is only a fallen angel. Unlike the devil, our Savior is omniscient and omnipotent; He is able to shield us, put a hedge about us, hide us in the palm of His hand, and keep us in His pavilion. He will deliver us from all the power of the devil, and preserve us in the enjoyment of that salvation He has purchased for us (Heidelberg Catechism, Q. 1).

6. We should be motivated by knowing that the duties to which the Lord calls us require more than what we can do in our own strength. We are to love the Lord with all our heart, mind, soul, and strength. We are to keep the Lord ever before our eyes and not covet our neighbor's wife or goods. We are to think upon things that are holy, just, and good. We must not give way to vain and sinful thoughts, but take every thought captive to Christ. We are to be truthful with our neighbor and season our words with grace. We must not allow any corrupt talk to come out of our mouths. We are to guard our hearts with diligence, and set our affections upon things above, where Christ is. We are to obey these commands not once or occasionally, but continuously. We are to obey God with all our might. In short, we are to be Christ-like in thought, word, deed, and emotion. All of this is impossible for us to do, yet the Lord calls us to nothing less.

How can we expect to obey God's commandments without Christlike zeal? When our strength fails so quickly here on earth, how can we expect to keep going into eternity? When we grow weary of our temporal duties so soon after setting our hand to the plow, how can we believe that weariness will not oppose us in our eternal duties? How can we grow in religion without zeal?

Indeed we cannot, for there is no true religion without zeal.[46] Zeal alone can sustain us with the heavenly strength and endurance of Christ, who is the Author and Finisher of our faith. Zeal is like faith; without it you cannot please God (Heb. 10:38–39; Rev. 3:19). In granting us zeal, God gives us strength and endurance beyond ourselves so that we may do what is required of us. If the Lord has called you to heavenly living, will you not look to Him for heavenly zeal?

7. We should be motivated by the great danger of coldness. Zeal is like the salt of the covenant (Lev. 2:13); it prevents putrefaction. Manton described the danger of living without zeal: "Not to go forward is to go backward. Standing pools corrupt; as a man that rows against the tide and stream, if he does not ply the oar, he will lose ground, and be carried away apace; so if we be not zealous we cannot stand and keep our ground."[47]

What makes this danger so great is that we have enemies without and within, which seek to quench our zeal and overthrow our faith. Outside are the devil and the world, besieging us with temptations and sore trials. Inside, we contend with our evil heart and the lusts of the flesh (Rom. 7:14–25). While we are in the body, we are at war. The danger is indeed great if we cease to watch, cease to pray, cease to fight against sin. Such unremitting warfare demands our zealous attention. The great dangers so near at hand should inflame our zeal day by day.

Where then is your zeal? Are the bellows blowing upon your first love, lest you forsake it (Rev. 2:4–5)? Have you set your affections above, where Christ is, lest they be seduced by the world below (Col. 3:1)? Are you being transformed by the renewing of your mind, lest you become conformed to this world (Rom. 12:2)? Are you zealous for Christian growth and maturity, that you may not be tossed to and fro and carried about by every wind of doctrine (Eph. 4:14)? If you are not constantly

---

46. Ames, 58.
47. Manton, "Zealous of Good Works," in *Works,* 16:289–90.

alert, your zeal may cool. Just as a fire will die if left untended and smothered by accumulating ash, your zeal may die within you unless you refuel and refresh it, keeping yourself in the love of God, and growing in the grace and knowledge of Christ (2 Pet. 3:18, Jude 21).

8. We should be motivated by realizing there cannot be too much zeal. "The least is more than enough in sin, because everything is too much there; but in grace there is never enough," wrote Manton.[48] Who among us can say that they have done enough for God, that they have put off enough sin and embraced enough duty? Who can say they have loved God and their neighbors to the extent demanded in the law (Matt. 22:37–40)?

"In the love of God, and zeal for God, and the service of God, and solid piety, there can be no excess; you cannot be too heavenly or too holy," Manton said.[49] In the light of God's love for us, the price paid for our sin, the pain suffered by Christ, and the great mercy shown to us, none of us has ever been zealous enough for God. The danger is doing too little, not too much. Manton wrote, "There are some that are afar off, that do not enter at all, that neither strive nor seek to enter, that are as swine, filthy, abominable, unprofitable, good for nothing but to ruin themselves, as profane persons and heathens; and some are very nigh to the kingdom of God, as the moral man upon the brink and border, and as he that was 'almost persuaded to be a Christian,' Acts 26:28. Others again make a hard shift to get to heaven; they are scarcely saved, or saved as by fire. But others are carried on with full sails, their hearts are enlarged to God. This is our duty, to labor to get this abundant entrance. Some seek to enter, and are not able; they go far, and yet perish: Luke 13:24, 'Many shall seek to enter, but shall not be able.'"[50]

How great is your zeal? Will you never enter God's kingdom because of your love of sin? Or have you almost been persuaded to be a Christian but hesitated because you feel secure with your own morality? Are you someone who hopes to enter heaven by moderation and compromise? Or are you possessed by such fiery zeal that you are cer-

---

48. Manton, "Zealous of Good Works," in *Works*, 16:290.
49. Manton, "Zealous of Good Works," in *Works*, 16:290.
50. Manton, "Zealous of Good Works," in *Works*, 16:290–91.

tain of being accorded an abundant entrance into the kingdom? The abundant entrance is promised to the diligent (2 Pet. 1:10–11)—what is diligence but persistent zeal? Where is your zeal?

9. Understanding the need for true zeal should motivate us to think how repugnant a lukewarm spirit is to God.[51] Can a lifeless, barren faith, or an indifferent, compromising spirit be the fruit of Christ's suffering, death, and resurrection? Is God pleased with such a faith or such a spirit in His children?

Either we are zealous for God or we are odious to God.[52] Where do you stand? Answer the following questions posed by John Reynolds:

- Did Christ descend into our mortal flesh, that we should be unconcerned whether we be translated from the world, and go to His glory, or no?

- Did He abase Himself, and make Himself of no reputation, that we might be made indifferent towards His name and honor?

- Did He employ thirty years on earth, in an unwearied zeal for His Father's glory, to excuse us from an emulous ardor in design and love?

- Did He lay down His life for our salvation, that we may be unconcerned, whether we are saved or no?

- Did He rise from the dead, and seat Himself in heaven, to excuse us from a solicitude about affairs, that are above, where He sits at the right hand of God?

- Has He told us of His resolution to return, and judge the world, that we may be secure, and negligent about the issue of that decisive Day? How *contradictious* to all His love and work is our lukewarmness in His ways? What ingratitude to Him is contained in the bowels of it? What contempt does it pour upon His blood and grace; upon His light and revelation; as if we looked upon them all as unnecessary, impertinent things?[53]

---

51. Reynolds, 209.
52. Manton, "Zealous of Good Works," in *Works,* 16:291.
53. Reynolds, 209–210.

Where then is your zeal? Are you so lukewarm in spirit that you invite God's rebuke? Are you indifferent about your readiness to stand before the Lord on the Day of Judgment? Are you blasé about the call to holiness, not caring whether you grow in the grace and knowledge of Christ, whether you put off sin, or whether you take up the duties He gives you? Manton said, "You do not worship the vanities of the gentiles, therefore be not [as they are, Ps. 115:4–8] dead, cold, and careless. You worship the living God, and he will be served with life, zeal, and strength of affection."[54]

Are you ready to stand before God in your lukewarmness? Are you ready to give an account of how you have used the talents He has given you? Are you ready to explain why you have squandered time, squandered mercies, squandered privileges, and squandered your life?

If not, where is your zeal?

Study Questions

1. Read Revelation 3:19. Christ commands us to be zealous. According to verses 15–16, how does Christ feel about those who are not zealous for Him?

2. In Luke 13:23–24 Christ said that to be saved we must "strive to enter" the kingdom. "Only those who strive with might and main, and whole-heartedly to enter, will be saved," writes Norval Geldenhuys. Why is energetic striving the only way to salvation? How is this different from trying to save ourselves by our good works?

3. Read Titus 2:14. What kind of attitude towards good works does Christ's death produce in His people? Think for a moment about how Christ "gave himself for us." How should meditating on Christ's cross energize us to serve Him? What kind of "good works" would His grace motivate us to do?

---

54. Manton, "Zealous of Good Works," in *Works,* 16:292.

4. How was Christ a model of godly zeal in His earthly life? How does His zeal display the beauty of loving God with all our hearts? How should we imitate Him, even if we are not called to be preachers?

5. What are some ways in which the devil and wicked people zealously pursue evil? Why don't believers pursue good with an even greater zeal?

6. Why do some people who have previously been lazy, suddenly shift into action when a deadline approaches? In what ways is time quickly running out for Christians to serve the Lord? How should that motivate us to work with all our might?

7. First Corinthians 16:13 speaks to us as to soldiers in a war. How does a soldier act differently in peacetime as opposed to war? Why? Are Christians to act like civilians in peacetime or soldiers at war? Why? See Ephesians 6:11–12.

8. Manton said, "In the love of God, and zeal for God, and the service of God, and solid piety, there can be no excess; you cannot be too heavenly or too holy." Do you think a person can ever be too zealous for the Lord? Why or why not?

9. Read Deuteronomy 6:5. What does God command? Is this the duty of all people, or just the super-spiritual? What does the repeated word "all" say about our zeal?

10. Which one of the many reasons listed why zeal is necessary for true Christian spirituality is most motivating to you? Why?

The Regulation of Christian Zeal

Religious zeal is regulated intrinsically by its own nature and character and extrinsically by the Word of God and other graces of the Holy Spirit. While counterfeit zeal has a selfish rule, blind zeal has a false rule, and turbulent zeal has no rule, sacred zeal has a sacred rule. Our aim in this chapter is to understand the need for regulating sacred zeal, then to examine its intrinsic and extrinsic regulation. We will conclude with considering the objections lodged against Christian zeal.

Why Regulate Zeal

After a brief definition of zeal in his sermon on Revelation 3:19, John Evans spoke of the need for regulation. He said of zeal, "Indeed it is no virtue at all, unless it be well placed and regulated. Zeal in its general notion is nothing else but a strong and ardent concern for or against a thing, and a lively and vigorous manner of acting thereupon."[1] In other words, without proper regulation, zeal is nothing more than passion let loose. The very thing that makes zeal sacred is its regulation by a sacred rule.

Evans went on to say, "It has the denomination of a *religious* zeal, only as far as the objects, about which it is conversant, are of a religious nature. And even a religious zeal is no farther good and commendable, than when it is really on the side of truth and goodness; when it

---

1. Evans, 320.

is measured by the importance of things, and when it is expressed and exercised by lawful and regular methods."[2] So to possess *sacred* zeal, we must not only be inflamed about sacred things, but also for sacred things in proportion to their importance, and exercised according to prescribed methods. Sacred zeal cannot stay within proper bounds without control or regulation.

Furthermore, if we consider the prevalence of false zeal in religion and the damage it can do, we should concede the need, not only for a wise rule, but also for a holy rule to govern religious zeal. Evans wrote, "It is fit to be observed, that we read in scripture of a *bad* zeal more frequently…than of a *good* one; and many admonitions are given against some sort of zeal…. [This] should make us sensible, how highly necessary it is, that a strict caution and a very careful regulation should attend our zeal."[3]

King David was zealous in conducting a census of his kingdom, despite Joab's warning (2 Sam. 24:3–4). David later repented of this sinful zeal (v. 10), but he could have avoided much painful punishment if his zeal had been regulated by a concern for God's glory instead of personal pride and ambition. Recall the zeal of Hezekiah in showing Babylonian ambassadors the treasures of his kingdom (2 Kings 20:12–15). From the account in 2 Chronicles 32:24–31, it appears that Hezekiah's success and prosperity had made him somewhat proud. His zeal was wrongly motivated by a concern that these foreigners and their king would think him worthy of their honor and gifts because of his great riches. His zeal should rather have been regulated by his concern for the emissaries' souls and God's honor; then Hezekiah would not have shown off his worldly goods but thought only about telling them about the true God of all creation, who by His almighty power had healed him of the very sickness that motivated their coming to see him.

We need not argue how inappropriate it is to be either overheated about small matters or indifferent about matters of great significance; both are universally acknowledged as unbalanced and inappropriate. Sacred zeal must be measured by the value and importance of things. It

---

2. Evans, 320.
3. Evans, 320.

should be suited to the need at hand and dressed for the occasion. Evans explained, "Zeal should bear a proportion to the 'value and importance of things.' Indeed, the least truth, of which we are convinced, must not be given up; nor should we act contrary to known duty in the least instance, upon any worldly consideration. But all truths or duties are not of equal moment or concern either to ourselves or others, to the honor of God or the interest of religion."[4] If that is the case, Evans said, "There is room for the exercise of moderation as a virtue, in relation to things of small consequence."[5]

Being overzealous about small matters and careless about significant matters can only result in hypocrisy. Evans said of this monstrous zeal, "Nothing indeed which appears to bear the stamp of divine authority, is to be received by us with an absolute indifference; but as God has laid a different stress upon things, so should we, and endeavor to follow his declared judgment of their importance, as near as we can."[6]

How can we know what bears the stamp of divine authority and what does not? If something bears the stamp of God's authority as a truth or a duty about which His people are to be zealous, how can we know how much stress He wants us to put on it? Such questions can only be answered by submitting to a sacred rule, for zeal must be regulated.

Benchmarks for Determining the Value of a Belief or Duty

In answering such questions, Evans suggested we consider two benchmarks.[7] The first is the Word of God, which, according to the third answer of the Westminster Shorter Catechism, principally teaches what man is to believe concerning God, and what duty God requires of man. Scripture alone has the authority to declare the necessary points of belief or practice in our salvation. If Scripture classifies something as a necessary belief (e.g., the resurrection of Christ, 1 Cor. 15:17) or an incumbent duty (e.g., forgiving one another, Matt. 6:14–15), that

---

4. Evans, 325.
5. Evans, 325.
6. Evans, 326.
7. Evans, 325.

belief cannot be maintained, that duty cannot be performed, with too much zeal. But if Scripture assigns the matter to the realm of Christian liberty (Rom. 14:1–3, 22–23), it would be wrong to be overly passionate about one side or the other. Matters of liberty call more for love than for zeal (Gal. 5:1, 13).

The second benchmark by which we may determine the value and importance of a belief or duty is its tendency to promote or hinder practical godliness, for we have been called to this as God's people. First Peter 1:15–16 says, "As he which hath called you is holy, so be ye holy in all manner of conversation; because it is written, Be ye holy; for I am holy." On the one hand, we may ask whether the belief or duty contributes to the promotion and defense of godliness. If it does, then with an eye to the glory of God and the edification of His people (1 Cor. 10:31; Heb. 10:24–25), we should zealously uphold it. On the other hand, we should ask whether the implementation of this activity or belief hinders practical godliness. If it does, then with an eye to the call of the gospel to devote ourselves unto good works (Titus 3:8; Eph. 2:10), we should be zealous against it. Sacred zeal must be regulated according to the dictates of a sure rule.

John Reynolds wholeheartedly agreed that "sacred zeal must have its guide and rule."[8] He said that without proper rule and measure, sacred zeal would forfeit both its name (zeal) and character (sacred). It would cease to be what it is and change into false zeal. Early in his discourse on zeal, Reynolds argued the need for a holy rule and its measure with two considerations: first, that sacred zeal is *zeal,* and second, that sacred zeal is *sacred.*

In considering zeal as zeal, Reynolds said that zeal, as a fire in a man's bosom, is the natural fervor of the human soul. What is more in need of rule and regulation? Reynolds explained, "The spirit of man…needs rule, as being of itself imperfect and blind, ready to mistake the most excellent, amiable objects; or, if they be at any time chosen and adopted, to mistake the way to the gratifying and to the enjoyment of them. What is naturally more irregular and exorbitant than the spirit of man? It is

---

8. Reynolds, 20.

abundantly impregnated with sinful dispositions and principles; and thence it is impetuously carried forth to all practical enormity."[9]

Reynolds said that when we consider zeal as the venting and operation of the spirit of blind, sinful man in the moral sphere, we need no other argument for its regulation, because such zeal consistently pursues pernicious and sinful objects, and jettisons all true and worthy objects. "When such [evil] objects and ends are cultivated and pursued, no wonder the means and methods subservient thereto are [just] as unworthy and improper; and so the whole process of human life becomes a disorderly, tragic scene, beginning ill, proceeding mischievously, and ending worse," Reynolds said. "Natural, unregulated zeal is an incarnate devil."[10]

That is a strong conclusion, maybe even shocking. But can we affirm any less when we see what unregulated zeal has done to people in Scripture? When Peter talks about people who were insatiable in their zeal for sin, he calls them accursed children who have forsaken the right way and gone astray (2 Pet. 2:14–15). When Paul writes of the Gentiles, in their lost, darkened state, he says that they "have given themselves unto lasciviousness, to work uncleanness with greediness"; such zeal for sin is to be put off by the Christian, as belonging to the old way of life (Eph. 4:17–22). Paul warns Timothy about Alexander the coppersmith, who in the manner of Satan, zealously opposed ("greatly withstood") Paul's preaching; but Paul was confident that the Lord would repay him according to his works (2 Tim. 4:14–15). Reynolds's conclusion that natural, unregulated zeal is an incarnate devil is not an overstatement. The sinful tendencies of human zeal necessitate regulation.

But what about *sacred* zeal; does this also need regulation, or is its sacredness enough? Reynolds said that zeal which is truly *sacred* is so in every respect: to its principle, object, end, exercise, and mode of operation. Unfortunately, such zeal is rare, even among Christians. Therefore our sacred zeal must be managed by a sacred rule and measure so that it is both genuine and sacred in its aim and actions.[11]

---

9. Reynolds, 67–68.
10. Reynolds, 68.
11. Reynolds, 69.

Another reason why regulation of sacred zeal is necessary is the presence of impetuous, exorbitant zeal. Reynolds often spoke of the damage caused around the world by "unevangelical, illegitimate zeal." "It is needful to call such a vigorous agent to regulation, and to consider by what Holy Rule it must be managed, that it may be *sacred*; and that being so in one respect, it may be uniform throughout and sacred in others also. It is very unnatural and absurd, that what is sacred in its design, supposed as aiming at God and His glory, should at the same time, be infernal in its immediate exercise and acts, as if it would play the devil."[12]

Oliver Bowles also contributed to this discussion of zeal. In his sermon on John 2:17, Bowles urged the Westminster divines to "put on zeal as a cloak" as they enacted church reform. He warned the divines that their zeal must be duly qualified lest it burn out of control like a wildfire. He said, "As mettle is dangerous in a blind horse, so [is] zeal when not directed."[13] Without a rule to guide it and a measure to keep it in bounds, zeal can pursue a dangerous and destructive course. A necessary rule adds light to zeal's innate heat, Bowles said. He warned that "zeal, as fire, must have light as well as heat. It is Hell where there is heat and no light but utter darkness."[14]

Sacred zeal needs a rule to lead it and to preserve it from degenerating either into foolish bigotry or irreligious zeal.[15] Even in Christians, sacred zeal cannot keep to a right path on its own; it needs a rule. Furthermore, to preserve its name and character as *sacred* zeal, it must have a *sacred* rule, for just as the zeal is God's, so the rule must be God's. Let us therefore consider the rule by which sacred zeal may be properly regulated.

The Intrinsic Rule of Sacred Zeal[16]

John Reynolds said that sacred zeal is regulated by both an intrinsic and an extrinsic rule, each of which has a twofold manner of governing.

---

12. Reynolds, 78–79.
13. Bowles, 25.
14. Bowles, 25.
15. Reynolds, 79.
16. This section is drawn largely from Reynolds.

Intrinsically sacred zeal is regulated by its nature and character. Extrinsically it is regulated by the Word of God and by the sacred graces that call for its exercise. When speaking of sacred zeal being regulated by its own nature, we may consider this in two ways: first, by its general nature as zeal, and, second, by its specific character as *sacred* zeal.

Human zeal is "the ardor and ardent exercise of a human spirit, the lively and vigorous egress of a rational soul towards an adopted object."[17] As such, zeal is rationally guided in choosing its object, directing it to adopt something worthy of the soul in which it dwells, and worthy of its zealous application and prosecution. In other words, man's soul necessarily regulates man's zeal. So if we are to consider the regulation of sacred zeal as human zeal, we must begin by considering the soul out of which it springs. If the human soul can serve as an intrinsic rule for its own zeal—though not *by itself*, to be sure, and though not *properly* in its fallen estate—then what can be said of the soul?

The soul by nature is a noble creation, with powers, capacities, and operations indicative of its noble Creator. The soul has a mind capable of extensive apprehension. It is able, within its creaturely limits, to reach to the heights of heaven, to the ends of earth, and into the depths of hell. It also has appetites and desires so large that nothing in the earth can satisfy them. But in its natural inclination to immortality, Reynolds said, "without a proportional, immortal satisfaction, [it] must necessarily sink beneath its own natural inclination and appetite."[18]

The native dignity of the soul is also seen in the body in which it dwells, for it is perfectly furnished to be a suitable habitation and a suitable instrument and outlet for the various operations of the soul. Moreover, this soul is placed in a world in which the Creator has wonderfully provided for the soul's contemplation and improvement. The soul is continually summoned by its surroundings to behold the wisdom, power, and beneficence of its Creator. Psalm 19 says, "The heavens declare the glory of God; and the firmament sheweth his handywork. Day unto day uttereth speech, and night unto night sheweth knowledge. There is no speech nor language, where their voice is not heard. Their

---

17. Reynolds, 80.
18. Reynolds, 81.

line is gone out through all the earth, and their words to the end of the world" (vv. 1–4). As the soul of man contemplates the world in which it is placed, it traces the works of nature up to their original, independent Cause until it is lost in admiration and delight at so wonderful a Creator. In short, nature, the physical body, and the world call man's soul "to view itself as the offspring of the great God, and to arise and salute its incomparable Parent, and congratulate itself [on] the nobility and honor of its Celestial Parentage."[19]

Imagine a soul that assists and propels sacred zeal; a soul that directs its zeal towards its divine Creator, which it is naturally inclined to do. Now imagine that God has given you such a soul that you naturally rise from creation to its Creator; that your affections are naturally directed to Him who is all-wise, all-good, all-sufficient, and all-glorious; and that your thoughts naturally dwell upon Him who is the immortal, invisible, and only wise God. The Lord our God has not left Himself without witness in the world He has created, nor in the creature made in His own image. Rather, He has declared that all mankind "should seek the Lord, if haply they might feel after him, and find him, though he be not far from every one of us" (Acts 17:27).

How inconceivably wrong it is, then, for us to prostitute our zeal and vigor by worshiping shameful things! Reynolds asked, "Shall a heaven-born [i.e., heaven-created] soul tend only downwards; and gravitate only to dust and clay! What is there here within the verge of the terraqueous globe[20] worthy the infinite propension[21] and effort of a comprehensive, endless soul? What are heaps of metal, airy honors, [and] sensual momentary pleasures, that they should pretend to be a match, meet for the amours and embraces of an incorporeal spirit? What affinity can it have with such things, were it not for the meditation of its terrestrial vehicle, which, in a little while, must be dropped in the dust?"[22]

When God breathed the breath of life into man's nostrils, man became a living soul (Gen. 2:7). God put into our earthen frame a soul

---

19. Reynolds, 81.
20. I.e., consisting of land and water.
21. I.e., inclination, disposition, or propensity.
22. Reynolds, 81–82.

that could only find happiness in communion with Him, in obedience to His ways. When Adam and Eve disobeyed the Lord, they severed that happy communion and brought upon the souls of all mankind incalculable misery (Gen. 3:16–19; Rom. 5:12, 15–19) and bondage to an evil master (John 8:34). Reynolds lamented, "Yet how degenerate are souls become, and unmindful of their state and pedigree! How justly may they disdain to be restrained and fettered within the confines of mortality! They should look about them and search out something excellent, spiritual, and everlasting, like themselves. What are fleeting shades and gaudy shows, to the substantial, permanent powers and inclinations of a spirit? What pity it is, [that] it should spend its heart and strength in the pursuit and clasping of a cloud?"[23]

How can we explain the things upon which our souls dwell? How can we excuse the desires and appetites that our souls embrace? How can our souls lose the sense of their immortality and holy parentage? The very nature of human zeal as the vigorous exercise of the heaven-created human soul has been perverted, and bent toward earthly objects.

"Awake, human souls!" Reynolds said. "Remember what you are, by whom made, and what you are made for! Reflect upon your native powers and excellencies! See what refinements, defecations [clearing oneself of the dregs of this life], and enjoyments you are capable of! And let not inferior, trivial things engross your study and prosecutions! Regulate your zeal by the consideration of the seat in which it dwells [and] the source from which it springs: an incomprehensible, inestimable spirit! Your nature should direct your affections to the most excellent and important objects."[24]

Our heaven-created souls must be urged away from the pursuit of the toys and trifles of this world toward the pursuit of "the most excellent and important objects." Anything less will sink the soul "beneath its own natural inclination and appetite." Left to its native blindness, the soul is incapable of contemplating and pursuing the most excellent and important objects. The nature of the human spirit in its sinful estate can only be renewed and refined by supernatural grace, which brings

---

23. Reynolds, 82.
24. Reynolds, 82–83.

human zeal under a double regulation, namely, "the regulation of that [new] *light* which dwells in the mind [and] the regulation of the new *principle* that now informs and actuates the heart; both lead the same way and dictate the same objects of zeal."[25] This shows the necessity of considering the specific nature of *sacred* zeal and how it acts as a regulator for our zeal.

In its human nature, zeal is the ardent exercise of the *human* spirit; in its sacred character, zeal is the vivid emanation of a *renewed and sanctified* spirit. Reynolds therefore concluded, "If a soul, as being a noble, deathless spirit in its own nature, ought, upon that very score, to aim at noble, immortal things, as the object of its ambition and zeal; what must regularly be expected from an anointed soul? One that has received an evangelical unction from above? Thereby, it is dignified with an additional excellency."[26] The Spirit changes everything in a man's soul. Pursuing the things of sinful flesh, or being zealous for them, leads to death, but spiritual-mindedness leads to nothing less than life and peace (Rom. 8:6).

To be sure, sin has rendered man's soul incapable of the ascent to God for which it was created. Human zeal will always be sinful zeal as long as men are by nature children of wrath (Eph. 2:1–3) and alienated from the life of God (Eph. 4:18). But when God saves us, He dwells in us by His Holy Spirit (Eph. 2:22; 3:16–17; Col. 1:27), renewing His image in us as the new man, "which after God is created in righteousness and true holiness" (Eph. 4:24). Mere human zeal can now become *sacred* zeal, and what would be merely the "ardor and ardent exercise of the fallen human spirit" becomes "the vitality and vivid emanation of a *sanctified* spirit saved by grace." The Holy Spirit enables the Christian to enjoy the double advantage of a sanctified soul and a sanctified zeal.

The Holy Spirit regulates the soul as an evangelical *light*, illumining our minds and directing our souls to the "most excellent and important objects" which lie above our terrestrial sphere. Reynolds described the Spirit's light as "evangelical," because it is promised to us in the gospel. He said it "scatters the clouds, and dissolves the mists of [our] dark,

---

25. Reynolds, 83.
26. Reynolds, 83.

benighted nature."[27] The Spirit's heavenly light reveals to our souls the objects that we should more properly and naturally pursue as persons born of God, who are not of this world, but are called to overcome the world (John 17:16; 1 John 3:9; 5:4).

Prior to the Spirit's enlightenment, the soul sees nothing more lovely and worthy of its zeal than this world (Rom. 1:22–23), but now another, better world is opened up to view (Col. 3:1–4). As a result, the beauty of this world, which once enamored us, almost vanishes by comparison. The great God, from whom we were once estranged by sin (Eph. 2:12), now appears in His majestic glory as the desire of our souls (Ps. 73:25). Moreover, Jesus Christ, the bridegroom of the new covenant, so fills the eye of the sanctified soul that it can scarcely look at anything else (Ps. 45:10–11).

Reynolds beautifully describes the heavenly devotion and zeal which the sanctified soul now exerts towards all things godly and by which it is regulated:

> The illuminated soul...wonders how it could waste its zeal and strength, as it has done, about vanities and delusions....
>
> Evangelical light ennobles and refines the soul; and then presents it with most suitable, worthy objects, for its most inflamed zeal. Particularly, it directs the soul to that supreme and summary One, *God in Christ*. There the conducted soul fixes, terminates, and rejoices; there it is filled, refreshed, and satisfied; there the zealous mind bounds its disquisitions and researches; yea, there it is lost in admiration and ecstasy. There the zealous heart, after all its pantings and defeats, finds utmost complacency and rest. God in Christ is worthy [of] all its ardors and amors; and nothing else can now appear to be so. It will now bless and applaud that Sacred Light, that opened its eyes, and so rationally, and so kindly guided it unto so transcendent, satisfying, blissful, and beautifying an Object.[28]

Indeed, sacred zeal makes the things of God to shine with a vigorous, attractive light to the eyes of the sanctified soul. It views the things of earth, which declare the glory of their Creator (Ps. 19:1), in the light of God's own glory, which now shines upon it. The things of this life,

---

27. Reynolds, 83.
28. Reynolds, 85.

which were once enchanting and desirable, now appear common in comparison to the glory of God in Christ, whose Spirit has renewed and filled the soul. The sanctified soul, which is risen with Christ, now zealously seeks the place where Christ is seated, at the right hand of God. How regulated that sacred zeal must be!

Who among us does not appreciate the blessed regulation of our zeal by the Spirit? Where would we be without His influence? For whom would our zeal be longing if not for the Lord of glory and His Christ? "Awake then, sacred souls! and see what claims your zeal! Will you act and strive beneath the dignity of your new nature and disposition? You are touched with a celestial flame; shall it be stifled or wasted upon earthly things?"[29]

How Sacred Zeal's Character Is Regulated

We have said that sacred zeal is regulated intrinsically by both its nature and its character. Having considered the regulation imposed upon it by its nature (for zeal cannot rise higher than its own nature), we now address some specific ways in which it is regulated by its sacred character.

1. Sacred zeal is regulated by the object upon which it fixes, and for whom it acts, that is, God in Christ and the affairs of His kingdom and glory. These divine and holy objects have a sanctifying influence upon the soul, for as the soul focuses upon divine things, "idols are thrown down [and] corruptions are mortified. The acts of this zeal are suited to the purifying objects, the modes and circumstances suited to the acts.... Sacred zeal will command the action and the circumstances of it that it may be such as is meet to be presented to, and performed for its excellent Object, the Blessed God."[30] In other words, the believing soul sends forth its zeal with an eye for God's glory and a heart for His commandments. These new desires regulate what arouses our zeal and how we express it.

2. Sacred zeal is regulated by the love of God. We love Him because He first loved us (1 John 4:19). Because of our love for God and His ways we

---

29. Reynolds, 86.
30. Reynolds, 91.

are zealous for good works (Titus 3:8) and against all evil (Ps. 119:113). Hence the *operation* of sacred zeal can be seen as the result of a holy love. This love is a regulation on what zeal pursues. Holy love terminates upon the holy God who dwells in unapproachable light (Ps. 18:1). From Him love goes forth to His incarnate Son, the Lord Jesus (Eph. 6:24). From Christ this love flows out to His church, His purchased bride (John 21:15), and into the hearts of all her members (Rom. 5:5). Finally, this love flows out to the world at large, and to specific souls within reach and view (2 Tim. 2:10). Operating under the domination of holy love, sacred zeal has a regulator which flows forth from God and His divine nature, which is love (1 John 4:8).

3. *Sacred zeal is regulated by its aim to honor and glorify God.* "Sacred zeal aims at the possession and enjoyment of the divine glory [which] it has chosen…for its inheritance and felicity," Reynolds wrote. "To that end, it aims here at exalting and spreading (as it can) the glory of its admired Lord."[31] Since God's glory is the aim of sacred zeal, its actions are necessarily regulated by God's glory in the means that zeal chooses to attain it. Sacred zeal rejects sinful means, the ways of ungodliness and unrighteousness, as unsuitable to attain and promote the glory of a righteous, holy God (Rom. 10:2–4).

4. *Sacred zeal is regulated by the Holy Spirit as its cause and author.* Reynolds exclaimed, "Now how excellent must that [zeal] be that descends from such a parent and original? What impression must it bear of its celestial author?"[32] Such zeal is holy, as God is holy (1 Pet. 1:13–16). It is intelligent and wise, for it comes from the Spirit of wisdom and truth (Isa. 11:2). It is full of goodness, love, and kindness, since such traits are the fruit of the Spirit (Gal. 5:22–23). It is spiritual, raised above earthly motives and concerns, because He is the Spirit of God and of glory (Phil. 3:3; 1 Pet. 4:14). In all these ways, the Holy Spirit regulates our zeal, so that it truly is sacred or holy.

---

31. Reynolds, 104.
32. Reynolds, 107.

5. Sacred zeal is regulated by its special office. According to Reynolds, sacred zeal is "a minister for God; an agent for heaven and the interests of it."[33] Sacred zeal keeps us alert to the enemy's designs, motions, and attempts. So the Apostle Paul can say that we are "not ignorant" of the enemy's devices (2 Cor. 2:11). Sacred zeal moves us to put on the whole armor of God and sustains us in fighting the Lord's battles (Eph. 6:10–18; 2 Tim. 4:7) against the adversaries of His crown and kingdom (Ps. 2:1–3).

"Thus we see what regulation sacred zeal would (and ought to) admit, from what has been called its *intrinsic* rule, or the several considerations that necessarily belong to its nature and character," Reynolds wrote.[34] Sacred zeal is intrinsically regulated, first by its nature, and second by its character. Its object is God; its operation, love; its aim, God's honor and glory; its author, the Holy Spirit; and its office, to fight sin and everything that opposes its adored object, the blessed God.

The Extrinsic Rule of Sacred Zeal

Along with its intrinsic rule, sacred zeal has the distinct advantage of an *extrinsic* rule, which is the Word of God. The Word of God is the inspired, inerrant, and infallible Scriptures of the Old and New Testaments (2 Tim. 3:16), which were written by men as they were moved by the Holy Spirit (2 Pet. 1:21). Zeal must have constant, submissive regard to these Scriptures, to refuel itself, and to maintain its sacred character. It must be animated and regulated by God's Word, giving full attention and obedience to every part of it. "Sacred zeal has a perfect written rule to direct its conduct, unto which it must continually look," Reynolds said. "Then shall I not be ashamed (of my way, or work, of my zeal, or myself) when I have respect unto all thy commandments."[35]

Other sacred graces, such as love, joy, peace, gentleness, and goodness (cf. Gal. 5:22–23) also act as extrinsic regulators of sacred zeal, for they are graces of the Spirit who indwells us. When a situation calls for any of these graces and zeal stirs it up for duty, the grace acts in a regulatory

---

33. Reynolds, 109.
34. Reynolds, 109.
35. Reynolds, 113. Cf. Ps. 119:6.

way upon our zeal. Zeal is then combined with that grace, as the situation requires, to constrain it to behave accordingly. In John 2:13–16 we see how Jesus' zeal combined with love for God's name and God's house. When the Lord's disciples reflected upon this, they attributed Jesus' extraordinary actions to His great zeal (v. 17), as foretold in prophecy (Ps. 69:9).

We also see how zeal combines with grace in Phineas in Numbers 25:6–8. His zeal for God incited him to take immediate action to punish sin and to avert a plague from Israel. The Lord Himself said that what motivated Phineas was his zeal for God (v. 13). Revelation 3:19 makes the same point when the Lord commands the Laodiceans to combine zeal with repentance. Thus, like the Word of God, other sacred graces provide an extrinsic rule by which sacred zeal is regulated and managed. Sacred zeal puts on needed graces as a cloak, dressing itself for the occasion, then responding to the need at hand.

Some Objections to Christian Zeal

We will conclude this chapter by answering some objections often raised against zeal in religion.

Objection 1: Do we truly need Christian zeal? Such a question seems legitimate, given how well much of the Christian church appears to be getting along without it. It would also be fair to suppose that when confronted with either a call for self-denial or some other display of true zeal, many people have indeed asked whether it is necessary to be *so* zealous for the Lord. It would also be fair to assume that such Christians have decided that zeal is not necessary and have opted for the cooler temperature of moderation. They think they are zealous enough and object to any more zeal in their religion.

Yet those who do not see zeal as necessary, or who think they already have enough of it and have become comfortable in their moderation, are usually the most vocal in their objections to zeal. Samuel Ward addressed several of these objections in his sermon on zeal.[36]

---

36. Ward, 84–86.

Some church members say, "What would you have us to do? We profess faith, go to church, and hear sermons, as good Christians ought to do." They see no need to be zealous about heart matters, but are only attentive to an outward show of religion.

Ward responds that it is also important to have zeal at home and in private, saying, "Such as whose families, closets, fields, beds, [and] walks do testify of their worship, as well as temples and synagogues, are right servitors [servants]. God much respects their devotions; and they have strong proof of the power of godliness."[37] In other words, as we learned in the last chapter, false zeal only concerns itself with an outward show of fruit before men. True zeal begins as a root in the heart and blossoms into the fruits of godliness, not to be seen by people, but to be offered to God in thankfulness. It is offered, not with a cry of "What more would others have us do?" but with a lament that so little has been done.

Objection 2: Will you have us outrun our neighbors or live without company? Some people fear becoming more zealous because it might cost them friends in the world. They think they might be labeled as overly religious or too different from others. They fear people's opinions more than God's. Ward's response to this was, "Cowards and cravens stand and look who goes first; but soldiers of courage will cast lots for the onset and fore-rank, for desperate services and single combats."[38]

Lukewarmness stands back and waits for another to take the hill to see whether the reward is worth the fight, the crown worth the loss of blood, and the blessing worth the cost. True zeal does not ask what others think, who will make the sacrifice, and whether others will join in. It does not wait for company when duty calls. Instead, it rises up at the clarion call and runs with haste to the Captain of the Lord of Hosts, saying with Isaiah, "Here am I; send me" (Isa. 6:8).

Objection 3: We will have danger and trouble soon enough; why should we invite it by being over-zealous? People who ask this question feel they have already suffered enough pain. They think they have been drained

---

37. Ward, 84.
38. Ward, 85.

enough of lifeblood and are loath to offer anymore. They have given up enough of life's pleasures and suffered enough of the world's reproach to invite any more.

Ward asked in return, "What danger can there be for an honest, peaceable, religious forwardness?" He went on to say, "The slug or snail puts out its tender horns to feel for lets in the way, and pulls them in where there is no cause; so do the fearful that shall be without; but zeal either finds no dangers or makes them none."[39] Moderation only makes those sacrifices in religion that self will allow. It measures and tempers itself to avoid threatened danger. True zeal fears no danger but focuses on a duty left undone. It sees obstacles as a demand for even greater zeal. Dangers do not quench true zeal but serve as fuel for its fire.

Objection 4: All people are not by nature as fiery a spirit as others. Why, then, should they seek to be what they are not? People with this objection to true zeal hide behind the claim that they are timid and quiet by nature, and moderate in spirit. They excuse themselves from increasing their zeal in religion, claiming they are just not the zealous type.

Ward's response to this is, "If there be such a dull phlegmatic creature, as hath no life or spirit in anything he goes about, or whom nothing will move, he may plead complexion; and yet grace is above nature. But the best way is, see every man compare his devotion in matters of God with his spirits and mettle in other affairs, wherein his element or delight lies. If the one equal not the other, the fault is not in nature: [for] the oldest man hath memory enough for his gold, and the coldest constitution heat enough where it likes."[40]

Lukewarmness looks for an excuse in nature, but grace can transform and enable nature to rise above itself. False zeal hides behind meekness of disposition, even though the same disposition readily gives itself with great zeal to the pleasures of this life. The falseness of this objection to increased zeal is exposed by the objector's uneven behavior; he is willing to be zealous in the things that suit his fancy, but lukewarm only in the things of God. True zeal, on the other hand,

---

39. Ward, 85.
40. Ward, 85–86.

concentrates all its affections upon God, and overcomes human weakness by becoming strong in faith and waxing bold for the Lord. It must be so since 2 Timothy 1:7 says, "God hath not given us the spirit of fear; but of power, and of love, and of a sound mind."

Objection 5: Not everyone has the time to devote to the study and work of religion. Time is a strange commodity. We all have the same amount of time, yet some accomplish so much more than others. One person's day is no longer than another's, but one spends his time more wisely than another. Yet some claim that they do not have the time to be zealous in their religion. They say they do not have enough time to attend church, search the Scriptures, read sound literature, pray, and use other spiritual disciplines more than they do.

Ward responds:

> There are indeed many vanities which distract and divide the mind of worldlings; but zeal counts one thing needful, to which it makes all others vail [yield] and stand by. Is there any so good a husband of his time, that will not steal some hour for his pleasure; that cannot spare his God and his soul half an hour, morning and evening; that bestows not idly as much time as a sermon or two would take upon in the week?
>
> The soul, I confess, hath a satiety[41] as well as the body; but why should we sit on thorns more at a sermon than at a play, think the Sabbaths longer than holidays, than want of zeal? If you would not be a vain and willing deceiver of thyself and others, deal honestly and plainly with thy soul, try thyself by these few rules; and if thou discover thyself to come short of them, amend and 'be zealous.'[42]

In other words, moderation cries out against the shortness of the hour because it looks only for time to satisfy its pleasure. We have enough time for what we most want to do, because we make time for it. True zeal is ablaze for God and therefore makes time for the things of God while it is yet day, because "the night cometh, when no man can work" (John 9:4).

---

41. I.e., the soul can also be filled to the point where it can receive no more for a time.
42. Ward, 86.

Why These Objections Fail

It should be clear by now that there is no substantial objection to becoming more zealous in our walk with God. All objections to religious zeal fail because they all stem from self-love and self-indulgence. They all rise out of an inordinate, sinful regard to self. They seek to pamper and please self, to protect it from harm or cost, and to guard its freedom. True zeal, on the other hand, seeks the death of self. Samuel Ward's plea for zeal in his sermon on Revelation 3:19 is an appropriate conclusion to these objections:

> It is good to be zealous in good things, and is it not best in the best? Or is there any better than God, or the kingdom of heaven? Is it comely whatever we do, to do it with all our might? Only uncomely when we serve God? Is mean and mediocrity in all excellent arts excluded, and only to be admitted in religion? Were it not better to forbear poetry or painting, than to rhyme and daub? And were it not better to be of no religion, than to be cold or lukewarm in any? Is it good to be earnest for a friend, and cold for the Lord of hosts? For whom dost thou reserve the top of thy affections? For thy gold?...
>
> Ought not all the springs and brooks of our affection to run [toward God]? May not he justly disdain that the least riveret [stream] should be drained another way? That anything in the world should be respected before him, equaled with him, or loved out of him, of whom, for whom, and through whom are all things? Who, or what can be sufficient for him, our Maker and Savior? In other objects fear excess; here no ecstasy is high enough.[43]

Study Questions

1. Reynolds said, "Natural, unregulated zeal is an incarnate devil." Why is zeal bad if it is not controlled by something greater than our natural impulses?

2. Read Matthew 23:23. Were the Pharisees zealous for tithing? Did Jesus tell them they should not tithe on their garden herbs? Why did He criticize them? Provide other examples of

---

43. Ward, 77.

being zealous for minor religious matters while neglecting the weightier matters of the Bible.

3. Read Matthew 6:32–33. What sort of things do the Gentiles zealously pursue? What does Jesus say we should zealously pursue? According to verses 19–20, what advantage does the one have over the other? According to verse 21, if we are zealous for earthly things, what will happen to our hearts?

4. God created mankind in His image. The Spirit breathed into us a rational soul. Christ saved His people for heavenly glory. How do we degrade ourselves if, like animals, we live only for earthly things?

5. Read Psalm 119:133. What is the rule by which the Christian must "order" his steps? What does the second half of the verse imply if we do not submit to this divine rule of obedience?

6. Into what forms of fanaticism might zeal lead a Christian if he does not regulate it by the Word? Could a sincere Christian fall into fanaticism? Why or why not?

7. What are some practical principles of the Bible that would regulate Christian zeal so that it would stay true to God's glory and man's good?

8. Read Galatians 5:22–23. How does each one of these fruits of the Spirit help to regulate zeal so that it remains true, holy, and beneficial?

9. How would you respond to the objection that zealous Christians are too fanatical and intolerant—indeed, too dangerous—and so "moderate Christianity" is better?

10. Imagine that someone you know wants to pursue God more zealously, but is afraid that his family or friends will think that he is strange or reject him. How would you encourage him to overcome that fear?

The Objects
of Christian Zeal

We will now consider four significant objects of Christian zeal. Because zeal is "the most intense degree of desire and endeavor to please and honor God,"[1] it will naturally show itself in the various spheres in which God's glory is concerned.

Speaking of the objects of sacred zeal, Reynolds wrote, "It relates to all things whereby the Church may be enlarged, edified, and advantaged…. Sacred zeal is an earnest desire of, and concern for all things pertaining to the glory of God and kingdom of the Lord Jesus among men."[2]

Reynolds also explained this broad expanse of sacred zeal another way, saying that when zeal culminates in God, in His perfections and glory, it may be called *divine* zeal; when it terminates in the Lord Jesus Christ, it is called *Christian* zeal; when it is most concerned with the interests of religion it is called *religious* zeal; and when it comprehends all of these, it is called *sacred* zeal. Our focus is on sacred zeal as the application of all our affections in the pursuit of the glory of God on earth, in life, in worship, and in the world.

The First Object: Glorifying God
Christian zeal strives to please and honor God in the intense pursuit of several objects *for His sake*, whether His glory and honor, personal holiness and growth in grace, the edification of the saints, or the salvation

---

1. Annesley, "How May We Attain?" in *Puritan Sermons,* 1:616.
2. Reynolds, 18.

of the lost. Christian zeal aims at such things for no other reason than they please God, glorify His name, and honor His saving work. In all it does, zeal has no more ultimate intent than to bring glory to God.

The Westminster Shorter Catechism contains 107 questions, which are divided into two concerns: what man is to *believe* concerning God, and what *duty* God requires of man. Question 3 explains that these are the principal things that Scripture teaches. Since God has revealed what man is to believe and what duty God requires of him, these are the necessary parameters of all biblical teaching.

But what is the motive of this instruction, both in the mind of the teacher and in the heart of the student? In other words, why should the teacher labor to teach the student what man is to believe concerning God, and what duty God requires of man, and why should the student labor to learn it? Why should such matters concern us?

The answer to these questions is found in the answer to the question with which the Catechism begins: "Man's chief end is to glorify God and enjoy him forever." We have no higher purpose in life than to glorify God because God created us, and all things, for His glory and good pleasure (Rom. 11:36; Rev. 4:11).

Despite this obligation to glorify their Creator, our first parents chose a different path; they sought to glorify themselves. They thought that this path would lead to enlightenment, and the status of divine beings ("gods") far above what God promised them as a reward for their obedience (Gen. 3:4–5). But this calculated act of rebellion against God only plunged them into misery, and a life of shame, fear, danger, hardship, debility, and death. Now they and their posterity were separated from God, the overflowing fountain of all good,[3] and of life itself (Ps. 36:9a). It also brought them and all their posterity into bondage to sin and self, a bondage fraught with temporal misery and eternal judgment. As a consequence, each one of us is born as a self-loving, self-seeking, self-centered, self-glorifying sinner (Pss. 51:5; 58:3; Rom. 3:10–18; 5:12, 19; Eph. 2:1–3), "prone by nature to hate God and my neighbor."[4]

---

3. Belgic Confession, Art. 1.
4. Heidelberg Catechism, Q. 5.

What then can be done? Can grace reverse the flow of the torrent of self-interest with which such a person is born? Yes, it can; indeed, *only* grace can. After Paul describes our natural deadness in trespasses and sins, and bondage to the devil, world, and our own sinful flesh (Eph. 2:1–3), he forcefully says in verse 4, "Sin has done all this to you; but God, who is rich in mercy, for His great love wherewith He loved us (before the foundation of the world!) has saved us by grace, quickening us, raising us up, and making us sit in heavenly places, together with Christ." What we could not do, God can do and has done, in Christ. Paul reveals God's great end in our deliverance: "That in the ages to come he might shew the exceeding riches of his grace in his kindness toward us through Christ Jesus" (v. 7). The God who made us for His glory has redeemed and renewed us for His greater glory, now and in the ages to come.

Salvation restores the believer to the relationship that Adam had with God prior to falling into sin (2 Cor. 5:18). It removes the enmity that sin imposed between man and God (Eph. 2:16; Rom. 5:9). We have peace with God through Christ (Rom. 5:1), and peace with one another in Christ (Eph. 2:14–16). We are freed from sin's dominion to live unto God, and to do all things to His glory (Rom. 6:11; 1 Cor. 10:31). Consequently, the Christian is reoriented in life, turned away from himself, from the world, and from the devil, and turned toward God. He wants God to be honored as the God of salvation; he desires God's friendship and fellowship, and he finds joy in doing God's will. In other words, the chief end of redeemed and renewed man is to glorify God, and to enjoy Him forever.

It is no wonder, then, that the Christian who is inflamed by sacred zeal pursues all those things which bring God glory. He has been miraculously reconciled to his chief end, his created purpose. So he is now zealous *for* all those things that will further God's glory and *against* all those things that may hinder God's glory. Little else attracts him because nothing else matters to him but the glory of the living God. All his affections are aflame in pursuit of this chief end. He minds the things of God as if he minded nothing else.[5]

---

5. Bowles, 6.

Can we, as Christians, do any less than pursue this chief end? Can we serve God in any other way than in the zealous pursuit of His glory? Oliver Bowles said there is "no such unbecoming evil as when the cause of God lies at stake, for men to be cold, lukewarm neuters, warping sometimes one way, sometimes another."[6] So the answer must be no. For Christ's sake, we are to put the interests of others above our own (Phil. 2:4), but the cause of God must be put above all else.

William Beveridge said it is impossible for us to serve God any other way than in zealous pursuit for His glory: "[Zeal] will certainly incline and move [a man] to employ his parts, his time, his power, his learning, his estate, and whatsoever talents God hath put into his hands, for His use and service.... It is impossible for us to serve Him any other way, than by laboring what we can to promote His honor and glory. That being the end of all His works, and the design that He Himself is always carrying on."[7]

Samuel Ward beautifully expressed this pursuit of God's glory, saying that Christian zeal "is a spiritual heat wrought in the heart of man by the Holy Ghost, improving the good affections of love, joy, hope... for the best service and furtherance of God's glory, [together] with... his word, his house, his saints, and salvation of souls."[8]

William Bates said that a Christian, who has by grace been restored to the pursuit of his chief end, must be principally zealous for God's glory, but this all-encompassing obligation and pursuit should be grounded on a deeper foundation than our creaturehood. For while God's work of redemption indeed restores us to the relationship with Him from which we fell, it does far more. By accomplishing our reconciliation through the work of an incarnate Savior, God has performed the part of a kinsman to us (Ruth 3:9; 4:14) and brought us into a filial relationship with Himself.

In other words, by salvation, God made us sons and daughters through the grace of adoption. Galatians 4:4–5 says, "But when the fulness of the time was come, God sent forth his Son, made of a woman,

---

6. Bowles, 8.
7. Beveridge, "The Duty of Zeal," in *Works*, 6:456.
8. Ward, 72.

made under the law, to redeem them that were under the law, that we might receive the adoption of sons." Upon this filial relationship sacred zeal grounds its obligation to pursue the glory of God above all else. It is *because* we are God's children by salvation and now love Him as our Father that we are zealous, no longer for our selfish glory, but for His divine glory. The cry of the child of God is ever, "Not unto us, O LORD, not unto us, but unto thy name give glory, for thy mercy, and for thy truth's sake" (Ps. 115:1).

Thus Bates stated, "A child of God is dearly concerned that His name be reverenced and magnified, His laws be observed, His worship maintained, that His interest be advanced in the world.... Those who with an indifferent eye see the cause, the truth, the interest of God depressed in the world, do renounce the title of his children."[9] Our adoption into God's family necessitates our zealous concern for promoting God's glory and our opposition to all that hinders it or obstructs it from view.

Ezekiel Hopkins argued that zeal (along with desire and joy) is an act of love for God that is called upon whenever God's honor and glory are at stake. His words are searching and convicting:

> The earnest desire of a true Saint is the enjoyment of God, and the glory of God.... Can he endure to see that God, whom he loves dearer than his life, daily provoked and injured? To hear his name blasphemed; to see his ordinances despised, his worship neglected, his servants abused, and the most sacred truths of religion denied, and the sacred mysteries of it derided? He is the most meek and patient man on earth, in his own concerns; unwilling to observe the wrongs that are done to him, and much more to revenge them; but when God is injured, the dear object of his love and joy, he can no longer refrain; but, whatsoever befall [God], [he] rises up to vindicate [God's] honor, and thrusts himself between to receive those strokes which were aimed at God; and what he cannot prevent or reform, that he bitterly bewails. This is true Zeal; and he that says he loves God, and yet is not thus zealous for him, is a liar.[10]

---

9. Bates, "Spiritual Perfection," in *Works,* 4:320.

10. Ezekiel Hopkins, "Exposition upon the Commandments," in *The Works of Ezekiel Hopkins* (Morgan, Pa.: Soli Deo Gloria, 1995), 1:275.

The sure way to know whether God is our God is to examine whether we are zealous when God is dishonored in any way, said Richard Sibbes. If God is our God, then we will love Him above all and pursue His glory above all. When He is dishonored we will not be able to sit still. Sibbes concluded,

> Whatsoever we make our god, we will not endure to have touched. If a man makes his lust his god, if that be touched, he is all in a chafe. When that which a man loves is touched, experience shows it, he is presently all on a fire. And here the best Christians have cause to be abased. Does God have their love, when they can hear him disgraced, and his name abused, without being greatly moved, and yet notwithstanding, in the mean time, will not endure their own credit to be touched, but they are, as I said, all on a fire? Where there is no zeal, there is no love. Certainly when we can hear God's children misused, and religion endangered, and profession scoffed at, and yet not be affected, nor cannot take God's cause to heart, this is great fault in our love.[11]

In short, if we have no zeal, we have no love, for zeal is the fruit and evidence of love.

To know whether God is our God, and whether or not we love God, we must examine our affections for God, to see whether or not we are zealous for His glory. Consider these questions from Hopkins:

> Are you jealous for the Lord of Hosts? Are your anger and grief never so much kindled for any wrongs that are done unto you, as they are for the provocations that are daily committed against the great Majesty of Heaven? Can you mourn and weep for these in secret; and, if you have power and authority to do it, punish and avenge them openly?—[then] you may, for your comfort, conclude, that certainly God has kindled this heavenly flame of Love in your breast: a flame that aspires heaven-ward; and will, at last, carry up your soul with it, and lodge it there where the Desire of Love shall be satisfied, the Joy of Love perfected, and the Zeal of Love eternally rewarded.[12]

A life that is not lived to God's glory is a wasted life. It is a squandered life for which we must one day give an account. Sacred zeal alone

---

11. Richard Sibbes, "The Faithful Covenanter," *The Works of Richard Sibbes* (Edinburgh: Banner of Truth, 2001), 6:11.

12. Hopkins, "Exposition," in *Works,* 1:276.

will set a Christian in pursuit of God's glory so that life might not only be *lived* to its fullest, but *enjoyed* to its fullest (WSC 1).

The Second Object: Our Growth in Holiness

If God's glory and honor is the chief object that sacred zeal pursues, then our own holiness must be a close second. It is true that if we pursue the glory of God, then nothing else need concern us, since that pursuit involves glorifying God in every area of life. However, to see what pursuing the glory of God in all of life looks like, it is important to discuss how Christian zeal inflames us to pursue personal holiness. This is principally shown in an ardent desire for light and knowledge.[13]

God's Word teaches first of all what we are to believe concerning God, so sacred zeal begins its work in us by inflaming our desire to know God and His Word. Compelled by zeal, we pursue Christ in all the appointed means of grace, longing to see Christ revealed in His Word, longing to hear Christ in the preaching of His Word, honoring Christ as Lord of the Sabbath day, joining with Christ to sing praise to our God in the midst of His church, availing ourselves of Christ's high priestly ministry by coming boldly to His throne of grace in prayer, and feeding on Christ in the Lord's Supper.

Sacred zeal makes us unsatisfied with how little we know when we come to Christ. It increases our desire to grow in the grace and knowledge of Christ (2 Pet. 3:18) and to mature from being children in the faith to becoming young men and eventually spiritual fathers (1 John 2:12–14). It makes us yearn to profit from the milk of the Word (1 Pet. 2:2) so that we might go on to enjoy the strong meat of the mature (Heb. 5:13–14), becoming not only a teacher of others (v. 12; 2 Tim. 2:1–2), but also most of all, an example to others (1 Tim. 4:12; Heb. 13:7).

Sacred zeal also compels us to labor for better knowledge of our duty, so that nothing that our Lord requires of us may be left undone; for clearer direction on our practice so that what must be done will be done well; for fuller instruction in the truths of the gospel that we

---

13. Evans, 328.

might always be ready to give an answer to anyone who asks a reason for the hope that is in us; for firmer persuasion of God's truth so we might zealously contend for the faith once delivered unto the saints; for a more forcible influence of God's Word upon our souls that we might not be conformed to this world, but be transformed by the renewal of our mind.[14] In other words, our zeal for knowledge stems from our zeal for holiness.

So inseparable from sacred zeal is this fervent pursuit of personal holiness that John Evans actually defined Christian zeal around it. He said,

> Christian zeal is the sprightly vigor, and strenuous activity of every holy affection and disposition; an earnestness and intenseness in every spiritual act, of faith and love, of hope and trust, of resignation to God and resolution for him. It is the performance of every act of devotion with life and close application of thought, as those who are in earnest in it; and with the exercise of those pious dispositions which are suitable to it. To praise God with admiring and adoring thoughts of his excellencies, with inward gratitude for his benefits, and with a lively sense of our own unworthiness; to confess our sins with a truly broken and contrite spirit, with a pungent shame and sorrow for them, and with vigorous resolutions against them…this is to be zealous in religion. To 'desire the sincere milk of the word, that we may grow thereby;' to come to all the means of grace with an aim to receive advantage by them, with a concern to exercise every proper holy affection in them, and to obtain acceptance of them; this is true fervor in devotion.[15]

In sum, the sacred zeal that is aflame in the heart of a Christian desires complete adaptation and conformity to the One whom we love.[16] Zeal's filial love for God is so great, and zeal's desire for God's glory is so great, that such zeal will accept nothing short of perfect conformity to His will. It therefore strives by all the means of grace to dress itself to the Beloved's liking. No duty is too costly that zeal will not take it up, and no earthly desire is so lovely that it will not be given up, to please its Lord. George Swinnock said, "Our work is not to make laws for ourselves or others, but to keep the laws which the great prophet of His

---

14. Evans, 328.
15. Evans, 328–29.
16. Reynolds, 26–29.

church has taught us; that coin of worship which is current amongst us must be stamped by God Himself."[17] With the apostle Paul, sacred zeal affirms, "I count all things but loss for the excellency of the knowledge of Christ Jesus my Lord: for whom I have suffered the loss of all things, and do count them but dung, that I may win Christ and be found in him, not having mine own righteousness, which is of the law, but that which is through the faith of Christ, the righteousness which is of God by faith" (Phil. 3:8–9).

Sacred zeal will not rest with a modicum of Christian duty, but neither will it cohabit with the smallest known sin, for it cannot be *for* duties which are pleasing to God without being *against* sins that are displeasing to Him. In its ardent desire to be completely adapted to the Beloved, sacred zeal cannot bear any lack of conformity, but loathes and laments it, desiring nothing more than to part ways, whatever the cost, with any sin that mars its beauty and displeases its Lord. Reynolds said that sacred zeal "grieves and mourns upon sight and feeling of each remaining imperfection and disorder. It breaks the zealous heart, that there are yet within her, disloyal, unkind, ungrateful dispositions and motions. She bewails her unhappy circumstances; grows impatient under them, and groans for deliverance and enlargement."[18]

Sacred zeal sees nothing more contrary to its enjoyment of God, communion with God, and conformity to God, than sin. Sin is the enemy, the power in the world most opposed to God, therefore sacred zeal hates sin with a perfect hatred.[19] Reynolds said that sacred zeal

> looks upon sin as the greatest, foulest, worst of evils. Its aspect therefore towards sin, is that of *hatred*. Such passionate form must *sacred zeal* put on, while it is here assaulted and annoyed by sin. It hates the *name* and *nature* of it, the *motions* of it within, the *temptations* to it from without. It is the chief or only object of its hatred; nothing else is so, any further than as it is infected with sin, or carries in it some inducement thereto. Such opposition to it is intimated and enjoyed in that call to seraphic souls, Psalm 97:10, 'Ye that love the Lord, hate evil!' The more you love Him, the more obliged you will be,

---

17. Swinnock, *Works*, 1:34.
18. Reynolds, 27. Cf. Ps. 120:5.
19. Cf. Ps. 139:21–22.

and inclined to hate evil, moral evil. It stands in fullest contradiction to that Lord of yours, to His will and Law, and glory. It is malignant to your souls; destructive to your delightful conversation with your Lord. No wonder then, we find a zealous soul professing his hatred of his own acts; so far as they are contaminated with this evil, and are thereby, displeasing, as being disagreeable to his beloved God, What I hate, that I do! Romans 7:15. Poor soul, that must carry about with him a hatred to himself and his own actions! As long as he is not perfect, but infected with this inherent evil, he must do so.[20]

Reynolds is right. No matter how intensely sacred zeal pursues conformity to its Beloved, the residual presence of indwelling sin ensures that perfect conformity will have to wait until death, which for the Christian is the abolishing of sin and our passage into eternal life.[21] But meantime zeal must strive to put off all known sin, for by God's grace it will not strive in vain. In this we can find no better comfort and encouragement than the promise of God to sanctify us wholly by the abiding, mortifying, and vivifying presence of His own Spirit within us. Ezekiel 36:27–29 should deepen our zeal to pursue conformity to God, for it shall be ours in the end: "I will put my Spirit within you, and cause you to walk in my statutes, and ye shall keep my judgments, and do them… and ye shall be my people, and I will be your God. I will also save you from all your uncleannesses."

Remember, too, George Swinnock's defining a godly man not by the *absence* of sin in his heart, but by his *unequivocal aversion* to the sin that remains there. It is our zeal to reflect God's glory in our own lives that engenders an aversion to all sin that we find in ourselves. Swinnock wrote, "In a godly man's heart, though some sin be left, yet no sin is liked; in his life, though sin may remain, yet no sin reigns. His heart is suitable to God's nature, and his life is answerable to God's law, and thence he is fitly denominated a godly man."[22]

---

20. Reynolds, 25–26.
21. Heidelberg Catechism, Q. 42.
22. Swinnock, "The Christian Man's Calling," in *Works*, 1:33.

The Third Goal: Strengthening the Soul and the Saints

Another object by which Christian zeal fervently pursues the glory of God is the edification of the saints. That translates into a high regard for the Lord's house, worship, and the Word by which the saints are edified, strengthened, and built up.

The zealous Christian takes seriously the biblical charge not to forsake "the assembling of ourselves together" (Heb. 10:25), because it is there, in the Lord's house, that God meets with His people and speaks tenderly to them (Exod. 25:22) through the appointed ordinances. It is in the Lord's house that the Word of grace goes forth in the gospel (2 Cor. 5:18–20). It is in the Lord's house that Christ's saving work is portrayed to nourish our weak faith (Gal. 3:1). It is there that the signs and the seals of the covenant of grace are administered for our growth in grace (1 Cor. 10:16–17). And it is there that the sweet communion and fellowship of the saints affords us a taste of heaven (1 Cor. 12:24–26).

For the zealous Christian there is nothing greater on earth than the worship of the triune God. It is in that worship that we join our voices of praise with the angels and the spirits of just men made perfect, as we draw near to God and His Son Jesus Christ (Heb. 12:22–24). It is the humble means by which we commune with the exalted and majestic Lord, rendering unto Him the praise and thanks that are His due. It is the means by which the saints join their voices together, calling upon God as one people, professing their faith, confessing their sins, lifting their eyes to heaven from whence their help comes, and raising their empty hands of faith to Christ Jesus, whose sufficiency alone can fill them.

Oliver Bowles said that worship is the means "whereby God and we have communion one with another [and] we do in a holy manner trade with God and he with us. This is *Jacob's* ladder, the angels of God ascend and descend by it; our prayers ascend, God's blessings descend. The ordinances are those golden pipes by which the golden oil empties itself into the hearts of God's people…they are the church's barn and wine-press; they are on Christ's part the kisses of his mouth, the mutual embraces between God and the Christian soul."[23] How can Christian

---

23. Bowles, 11.

zeal not be aflame for such a heavenly oasis on earth as worship? In worship we taste and see that the Lord is good (Ps. 34:8).

We must also be fervent in our zeal for the Lord's Word, for it is in the Word that God speaks to and edifies His people. Worship is a dialogue between heaven and earth, between God and His people. We cry out for help, and God responds with the promise of His presence; we cry out in confession, and God responds with an assurance of pardon; we cry out in prayers for guidance, and God responds with His Word. We cry out for blessing, and God responds with His benediction. All throughout worship, no matter what our need, no matter what our cry, we are directed again and again to the Word of God. It is the sovereign remedy and saving balm for the people of God.

Nothing but the utmost zeal for the Word of God could have led David to write Psalm 119, in which he praises God's Word in virtually every verse. So we too, when inflamed by sacred zeal, will fix our eyes on His commandments (v. 6), learn His righteous rules (v. 7), store His word in our hearts (v. 11), meditate upon His precepts (v. 15), put false ways far from us (v. 29), choose the way of faithfulness (v. 30), set His rules before us (v. 30), run in the way of His commandments (v. 32), delight in His commandments (v. 47), turn our feet into the way of His commandments (v. 52), hold back our feet from every evil way (v. 101), hate every false way (v. 128), rejoice at His Word like one who has found great spoil (v. 162), and not forget His commandments (v. 176).

Are we zealous for God's house, worship, and Word? Do we love His ordinances which are appointed for the edification of the saints? Are we zealous for His sanctuary, and do we long for His courts? Is His voice the voice of our Beloved? Have we seen God's beauty in His sanctuary and felt the comforts and delights of His house? Then we cannot forsake regular attendance in worship. We must be able to tell others what the Lord has done for our soul (Ps. 66:16), in what graces we have been strengthened (Eph. 6:10–18), and with what comforts the Lord has consoled our heart (2 Cor. 1:3–5). Do we love worship by which we commune with God and He with us? Then we will prize the Lord's Day and keep it holy, for it is the queen of our days, the oasis of our week, our refuge and reorientation.

Do we love the Lord's Word? Is it our divine cordial, our refuge, our rule and guide, our delight? Then we will not neglect to sit under its ministry. We will not neglect to heed its voice. We will not take lightly what the Lord says to us in it. In short, we will be zealous for the edification of the saints by these prized and glorious means of God's house, God's worship, and God's Word.

How shameful it is when we are cold toward the Lord's house and ordinances, unmoved by the apostolic greeting announcing the Lord's grace and mercy toward us, unmoved by the festal song that calls us to draw near to the Lord by announcing the Lord's drawing near to us. We should be shaken by our coldness to the call to profess our faith and renew our engagement to be the Lord's, by the call to confess our sin that we might receive assurance of the Lord's gracious pardon. It is sin to be unmoved by the proclamation of the Word of God which calls us again to find refuge in Christ and Him crucified, unmoved by the benediction which announces the Lord's blessing and favor upon all who trust in the Savior whom He has provided for us.

Only by sacred zeal can we say with the psalmist, "How amiable are thy tabernacles, O LORD of hosts! My soul longeth, yea, even fainteth for the courts of the LORD: my heart and my flesh crieth out for the living God. Blessed are they that dwell in thy house: they will be still praising thee. Selah. For a day in thy courts is better than a thousand. I had rather be a doorkeeper in the house of my God, than to dwell in the tents of wickedness" (Ps. 84:1–2, 4, 10). May God therefore restore to us the pursuit of His glory in the edification of the saints, beginning with ourselves.

But we should also strengthen our own souls through worship and other spiritual disciplines so that we can be of more service to the saints. Strengthening our own souls through the exercise of sacred zeal will enable us to grow in our zeal to strengthen our brethren. This calls to mind the many duties—too many to mention here—that Christians owe each other in the communion of saints. These are well summarized in all the horizontal imperatives in Paul's and John's epistles that focus on "one anothering." True, sacred zeal never ends in self and in God alone, but also reaches out to pray for and to show love to one another. The more zeal we have the more we will love the brethren and the more we will use the gifts God has given us for the well-being of the body of Christ.

The Fourth Goal: Saving the Lost

The zealous Christian affirms with the apostle, "I am not ashamed of the gospel of Christ: for it is the power of God unto salvation to every one that believeth; to the Jew first, and also to the Greek" (Rom. 1:16). He declares with the apostle, "Now then we are ambassadors for Christ, as though God did beseech you by us: we pray you in Christ's stead, be ye reconciled to God" (2 Cor. 5:20). He cries with the prophet, "Ho, every one that thirsteth, come ye to the waters, and he that hath no money; come ye, buy, and eat; yea, come, buy wine and milk without money and without price. Wherefore do ye spend money for that which is not bread? and your labour for that which satisfieth not? hearken diligently unto me, and eat ye that which is good, and let your soul delight itself in fatness" (Isa. 55:1–2).

It is not enough for sacred zeal that we ourselves know the Lord or that our fellow saints know the Lord; it is also imperative that all nations and peoples hear of Him, as He is preached in the gospel. Those who are lost must hear that there is salvation in Christ; the blind, that there is eye-salve in Jerusalem; the wounded, that there is a balm in Gilead. Sacred zeal longs and prays and labors for the day when all nations shall flow into the house of God, when the Word of the Lord shall be faithfully spoken from every pulpit. It yearns for the time when many shall come from all the nations of the world, saying, "Come ye, and let us go up to the mountain of the LORD, to the house of the God of Jacob; and he will teach us of his ways, and we will walk in his paths" (Isa. 2:3).

William Beveridge said that true zeal cannot help but be zealous for the promotion of God's glory among the lost. He wrote,

> true zeal for God will…put us upon…promoting His honor and glory, as far as we can in all other places. And seeing His glory… shines forth most gloriously in the way that He has made for the salvation of mankind, and revealed in His glorious gospel…if we have any zeal for His glory, it will appear in striving all we can to spread and propagate His said Gospel…that all nations may know Him,

and serve Him, and worship Him, and give Him thanks for His great glory manifested in their redemption, and so partake of it themselves, to their eternal happiness and salvation…. And therefore all who are truly zealous for His honor, cannot but be so likewise for the salvation of all men.[24]

Our zeal to promote God's glory by making Him known in the world will manifest itself in various ways. It will make us pity the condition of the lost, and how distant they are by their sin from their Creator, the Redeemer, and the sacred life of which they are capable (Rom. 9:1–5). It will make us lament their slavery to sin, knowing there is no way for their reconciliation and recovery to God without the gospel (Rom. 9:2). We will be driven to our knees praying that they may be brought to know the only true God and His Son Jesus Christ (Rom. 10:1). And we will be compelled to do all we can for the lost, striving to win those who are near and supporting efforts to win those which are far, believing it to be the highest service we can ever do for our Lord and His glory (1 Cor. 9:19–23).[25]

Likewise, such concern for the lost will inflame our zeal for good works. Christian zeal seeks to glorify God by doing good works, and especially by doing good to others in His name. "Let your light so shine before men, that they may see your good works, and glorify your Father which is in heaven" (Matt. 5:16). We do good works "that God may be praised by us…and that by our godly conversation others may be gained to Christ."[26] Christian zeal considers that whatever is done for the least of our fellow human beings is done unto Christ: "For I was an hungered, and ye gave me meat: I was thirsty, and ye gave me drink: I was a stranger, and ye took me in: naked, and ye clothed me: I was sick and ye visited me: I was in prison, and ye came unto me" (Matt. 25:35–36). Christian zeal agrees with James: "Even so faith, if it hath not works, is dead, being alone" (James 2:17); and in particular, Christian zeal is forward to "remember the poor" (Ps. 41:1; Gal. 2:10).

---

24. Beveridge, "The Duty of Zeal," in *Works,* 6:455–56.
25. Beveridge, "The Duty of Zeal," in *Works,* 6:456.
26. Heidelberg Catechism, Q. 86; "conversation" means "manner of life."

Personal holiness, the edification of the saints, and the salvation of the lost are all appropriate expressions of our principal object in sacred zeal, which is to glorify God on earth, in this life, in the fellowship of His church, and outside, in the world. Are you zealously pursuing these several ways of achieving your *chief end*? May God incline us and empower us, and glorify Himself in us, not merely as creatures, but as His adopted children. "For of him, and through him, and to him, are all things: to whom be glory for ever. Amen" (Rom 11:36).

Study Questions

1. Read 2 Corinthians 5:15. How does Christ's saving death change what we live for? How does it redirect our zeal?

2. Bates wrote, "A child of God is dearly concerned that His name be reverenced and magnified, His laws be observed, His worship maintained, that His interest be advanced in the world." Why are God's children concerned about His glory?

3. Hopkins said, "Are you jealous for the Lord of Hosts?" What are some things in our world that should offend us if we are zealous for God? What are the right ways to respond to such offenses?

4. Read Matthew 5:6. Hunger and thirst are intense, even painful, desires. Why does zeal for God's glory make us hunger and thirst to live in righteousness?

5. John Evans said, "Christian zeal is the sprightly vigor [active or lively strength], and strenuous activity of every holy affection." How does someone who is "on fire for God" act differently from the typical professing Christian?

6. Read Psalm 97:10. If our love for God is zealous, how will we relate to sin? How will that impact the way in which we respond to temptations?

7. Read Psalm 84:1–4. What was the psalmist so excited about? Why is the "house" or gathered church of God such a lovely place to be?

8. Oliver Bowles said that the divinely ordained means of worship "are on Christ's part the kisses of his mouth, the mutual embraces between God and the Christian soul." How would it change our view of public worship if we saw it as the opportunity to spiritually embrace Christ and be kissed by His Spirit?

9. Read Psalm 96:3. What does this Psalm call upon us to do? How can God's glory, majesty, and beauty (vv. 4–6) motivate us to this mission?

10. Beveridge said, "If we have any zeal for His glory, it will appear in striving all we can to spread and propagate His said Gospel…that all nations may know Him, and serve Him, and worship Him." How can you exercise your zeal for spreading God's gospel and kingdom?

The Outworking
of Christian Zeal

Let us now discuss what the zealous pursuit of God's glory looks like, according to the circumstances of our lives, and in various callings. For we are all bound by God to be faithful wherever He places us, making the most of the opportunities He gives us to show our love for Him and our zeal for His glory.

Scripture Teaching on Zeal in the Pursuit of One's Calling

Let us consider two passages from Scripture that show how zealously Christians are to embrace and pursue their calling in life. When John the Baptist was heralding Christ's coming with a call to repentance, many people came to him to be baptized, expressing their desire to turn from their sinful ways and prepare themselves for the arrival of God's kingdom. Merely coming to John to be baptized was not enough; John also charged these people to "bear fruits meet for repentance" (Luke 3:8, KJV margin, n. 1). They were to express their repentance with appropriate fruits or changes that would prove the sincerity of their coming to John for baptism and their desire to promote God's kingdom.

These people came from all walks of life, so John gave them specific instructions suitable to each of their situations. "And the people asked him, saying, What shall we do then? He answereth and saith unto them, He that hath two coats, let him impart to him that hath none; and he that hath meat, let him do likewise. Then came also publicans to be baptized, and said unto him, Master, what shall we do? And he said unto them, Exact no more than that which is appointed you. And the soldiers likewise demanded of him, saying, And what shall we do? and he said unto them, Do violence to no man, neither accuse any falsely; and be content with your wages" (Luke 3:10–14).

Paul makes the same point in Titus 2:1–10. He charges young Titus to call saints to a way of life that reflects and honors the great truths[1] of the gospel of Jesus Christ. He calls them to a life of *practical* righteousness for Christ, which agrees with their *positional* righteousness in Christ. Not content to lay a general charge upon Titus, Paul proceeds in the next verses to describe what practical righteousness looks like in various stages and stations of life among the saints, old and young, male and female, free men and bondsmen. Titus should teach:

> That the aged men be sober, grave, temperate, sound in faith, in charity, in patience. The aged women likewise, that they be in behaviour as becometh holiness, not false accusers, not given to much wine, teachers of good things; that they may teach the young women to be sober, to love their husbands, to love their children, to be discreet, chaste, keepers at home, good, obedient to their own husbands, that the word of God be not blasphemed. Young men likewise exhort to be sober minded…. Exhort servants to be obedient unto their own masters, and to please them well in all things; not answering again; not purloining, but shewing all good fidelity; that they may adorn the doctrine of God our Saviour in all things (vv. 2–6, 9–10).

These two passages affirm that while the call to live for God's glory extends to us all, there are also expectations peculiar to each believer's station in life and daily work, and therefore specific ways in which God is to be glorified. Let us therefore consider four callings in life: the minister of the Word, the laborer, the parent, and the private Christian, in terms of the effect that Christian zeal is to have upon each.

Zealousness in Particular Callings in Life

Calling #1: The Minister of the Word

The call to the ministry of the Word and sacraments is the highest calling of all. The Puritans would agree with the "Form of Government"

---

1. "The things which become sound doctrine" (Titus 2:1).

in the old PCUSA's constitution which says, "The *pastoral* office is the first in the church, both for dignity and usefulness."[2] The pastor speaks for God to the people, and to God on behalf of the people. He cares for the flock of God, in Christ's name and for Christ's sake, as His under-shepherd. This high calling should not be entered into lightly, and cannot be faithfully performed without the utmost zeal.

The minister is to give the most serious consideration to the work, weight, and goal of his office. He is to be mindful that his *work* as an ambassador of the gospel of Christ (2 Cor. 5:18–20) is the fulfillment of the great purpose of God from before the foundation of the world (Eph. 1:4). For God's eternal purpose was that Christ should redeem a people for Himself, and that the Father should adopt them as Christ's brethren and fellow heirs of the kingdom (Eph. 1:6–12; Gal. 4:4–6; Rom. 8:16, 17, 29).

It is true that the Lord uses many instruments to bring about His will. He used Assyria as a rod to chastise His people (Isa. 10:5), and Cyrus as a right hand to deliver them (Isa. 45:1–5). But no instrument that God uses in this world to bring about His will can compare to what He does by a minister of the Word. For the Lord uses a minister to speak to His people (1 Thess. 2:13), bless His people (Num. 6:22–27), teach His people (Isa. 54:13; 2 Tim. 4:1–2), and lead His people (1 Cor. 11:1; Heb. 13:7).

Great was the work of creation, in which God made all things out of nothing by the power of His word. He created everything in six days, and all very good (Gen. 1:1; Neh. 9:6; John 1:1–3; Rom. 4:17; Heb. 11:3; Rev. 4:1).[3] Yet greater was the work of redemption by which the Lord went down to Egypt and delivered His people from bondage. God brought judgment not only upon those who held Israel captive, but also upon their gods, showing them to be nothing and Himself to be the one, true, and living God (Deut. 4:32–39; Num. 33:4; Jer. 10:10).

But far greater still was the sending of God the Son into the world for us and for our salvation, as the Word of God incarnate, the Lamb of God who takes away the sin of the world, the risen Christ. This

---

2. "Form of Government," *The Constitution of the Presbyterian Church in the United States of America* (Philadelphia: Presbyterian Board of Publication, 1839), 408.

3. Cf. Westminster Shorter Catechism, Q. 9.

indeed was God's greatest work. It was His *new* work in the earth (Jer. 31:22), not only because of Christ's great condescension (Phil. 2:5–8) or because of the new and eternal union of the divine and human in one person (John 1:14; 1 Tim. 2:5), but because this latter work occasioned the first two. In the mind of God, who sees the end of His works from the beginning (Isa. 46:10; Acts 15:18; Eph. 3:9; 2 Thess. 2:13), it was this work of creating an elect family for Himself, a people chosen and precious, that generated the creation of all things and the incarnation of His Son as Redeemer (Eph. 1:5).

How great, then, is a minister's work! He is an ambassador of the purpose that first arose in the mind of God in His determination to create a world of men, who would fall into sin, and to incarnate His only Son as Mediator and Redeemer.

A minister is also to be mindful of the *weight* of his office in God's church as one of "the ministers of Christ, and stewards of the mysteries of God" (1 Cor. 4:1). Paul exhorts church members to "obey them that have the rule over (KJV margin: guide) you, and submit yourselves: for they watch for your souls, as they that must give account" (Heb. 13:17). Every minister of the Word must indeed give an account of his labors for the welfare of those to whom he is sent. James cautions men to think twice before offering themselves for the ministry of the Word: "My brethren, be not many masters, knowing that we shall receive the greater condemnation" (James 3:1). If faithful pastors who have served the Lord with readiness of mind, laboring diligently in the Word and in doctrine, preaching the Word in season and out, can expect to receive "a crown of glory that fadeth not away" (1 Pet. 5:4), what will Christ say and do to men who were slack or half-hearted in their labors, or else self-indulgent, abusing their office for their own pleasure or profit?

What Oliver Bowles said about the Westminster divines as church reformers was only true of them *as* ministers of the gospel and the Lord's instruments for the care of His church, which He purchased with His own blood (Acts 20:28). Bowles said,

> The Church is God's Garden, which being planted with all variety of flowers is apt to be overgrown with weeds, that not only mar the beauty of it, but eat out the good herbs. Reformers, their work

is to weed the Lord His garden, throw out all those noisome herbs which would have spoiled all the good ones (Song of Songs 4:12). The Church is the Lord's Orchard, wherein trees of all kinds, both for fruit and medicine, grow upon the banks thereof. The Master of that Orchard is impatient of any such trees that cumber the ground and after many years bear no fruit.

Reformers, their work is to root out the plants that God never planted (Song of Songs 4:13). The Church is God's House, where He delights to dwell. Reformers are to cast out all the dirt, dross, and garbage that is odious and irksome to the Master of the House; they sweep down all the cobwebs wherein the spiders did build (Heb. 3:6).

The Church is God's Spouse, in whose beauty His soul delights. That she should be deformed with strange attire, ornaments borrowed from notorious strumpets, the Lord cannot endure. Reformers they strip her of all her harlotry attire, take off all her Jezebel-like paintings, and render her to Christ in her native simplicity (Song of Songs 4:12).

The Church is the Lord's Vineyard, which He keeps and waters every moment. Reformers, their work is to take the foxes that destroy the vines (Song of Songs 8:12; 2:15). How welcome should the feet of such be? And how should the precious nature of the work in relation to God, draw out all our strength?[4]

How great, then, is the weight of the minister's office! The relationship God bears to His church through the minister and the obligation which the minister has to God for his work are unparalleled.

The minister of the Word is also to be mindful of the *end* of his function as the means by which the elect are saved. God created out of nothing, but God saves by means. The minister functions as God's herald to proclaim the good news of salvation for all who believe (Isa. 40:1–2). He declares, in the name of the King, the free offer of remission of sins and life eternal to all who believe on the Lord Jesus Christ (Isa. 55:1–7).[5] He is God's ambassador to appeal to listeners to be reconciled to God (2 Cor. 5:20). He is Christ's undershepherd, feeding the flock of God (1 Pet. 5:1–4) and taking care of the church, as a man rules his own house (1 Tim. 3:5), "warning every man, and teaching every man in all wisdom, that we may present every man perfect in Christ Jesus" (Col. 1:28).

---

4. Bowles, 9–10.
5. Heidelberg Catechism, Q. 66.

In Romans 10:13–17, Paul places the minister's work in its proper redemptive context, saying, "For whosoever shall call upon the name of the Lord shall be saved. How then shall they call on him in whom they have not believed? And how shall they believe in him of whom they have not heard? And how shall they hear without a preacher? And how shall they preach, except they be sent? As it is written, How beautiful are the feet of them that preach the gospel of peace, and bring glad tidings of good things! But they have not all obeyed the gospel. For Esaias saith, Lord, who hath believed our report? So then faith cometh by hearing, and hearing by the word of God." How great, then, is the minister's function as the means for gathering God's saints!

How can a minister fulfill so high a calling without zeal? With such great work to do, laboring under such a weight of sacred obligation, with such a high end in view, woe to the man whose heart is not fully engaged in his work, whose conscience is not captive to the obedience of Christ, who does not devote himself wholly and unstintingly to his Master's business, and whose aim is anything less than the glory of God, the edification of His church, and the salvation of sinners.

Consider, then, the effect of sacred zeal upon a minister. It sets him upon diligently fulfilling the ministry committed to him (2 Tim. 4:5). It gives him a tender love for souls and the will to labor for their salvation (1 Cor. 9:22). It moves him to instruct the ignorant (1 Tim. 4:11), rebuke the profane (Titus 1:9–13), encourage those who are hungry for Christ (2 Cor. 5:20), settle the wavering (Titus 2:1), revive the despondent (1 Tim. 4:16), restore the penitent (2 Cor. 2:6–8), confirm the brethren (1 Tim. 4:6), and fervently intercede for the flock entrusted to him (Col. 4:12–13).[6] Such duties are required of the minister, whether he is zealous or not—but how *impossible* they must be if he is cold to his calling!

Sacred zeal compels the minister to prepare his messages for immortal souls, mindful that this may be the last sermon they hear. This might be their final call to faith, their final word of comfort, their final word of assurance. Thus sacred zeal will incite the minister to

---

6. Reynolds, 163–64.

choose his text, refine his matter, adorn his method, and inflame his heart so that "Jesus Christ and him crucified" (1 Cor. 2:2) might be his sole proclamation. Sacred zeal will urge the minister to disdain overly academic language in the pulpit as much as flippant jesting. Because he is zealous for the Lord, zealous for the saints, and zealous for the lost, he will disdain the eloquence of the pedant as much as the joking of the comedian. He sees the pulpit as a place of reverence from which the Word of God goes forth, and as a place where he must give the strictest account (James 3:1–2; Heb. 13:17).

Moreover, sacred zeal urges the minister to preach with his life as much as with doctrine, in common conversation as much as in pulpit application. It urges him to cultivate friendship with the flock so that he might serve among them and be an example of living the gospel which he proclaims. It inflames him to pursue personal holiness and be diligent to do whatever promotes the glory of God. Private prayer for himself and his flock (1 Sam. 12:23) warms his heart. Sacred zeal compels him to preach in God's name, live to God's glory, and labor for God's church, so that by God's grace, souls entrusted to his care will not be lost (John 17:12).

In short, the zealous minister is ever mindful that he is many things: a herald, a servant, a steward, an ambassador, an athlete, a workman, a builder, a teacher, a shepherd, a husbandman, an overseer, a watchman, and a soldier. He remembers these biblical names and titles that remind him of the duties that God has entrusted to him, lest in forgetting those titles, he forget his duties, and lest in forgetting his duties, his titles be the ground of his accusers, and of the Lord's quarrel against him on the day when he must give an account of his calling (2 Cor. 5:10; James 3:1).[7] How the minister needs sacred zeal! And what effect it will have upon his labors! What is a minister without zeal but a danger to those he serves, and to himself?

Calling #2: The Daily Worker

The daily worker and wage earner also needs sacred zeal, for he must spend many hours in the workplace each week, in many cases shoulder

---

7. Bowles, 42.

to shoulder with unbelievers. He must obey his employer and superiors, and submit to decisions that have been made for him, in the company's best interest. His chief duty is to give an honest day's work for an honest day's wages. He should arrive for work on time, rested and ready to give his best effort to the work of the day. He must do his best at whatever task he is given, cheerfully cooperating with his fellow workers, looking out for his employer's best interests while cherishing a wholesome regard for the safety of the workplace and the needs of his coworkers. How can a Christian work in such an environment, and remain faithful to his Lord, his family, his church, and his own soul?[8]

First, remember that the laborer's calling is honorable before God. The Reformers and Puritans argued for the priesthood of all believers. They renounced the idea that a sacred calling alone was honorable to God (1 Pet. 2:9). All lawful vocations are from God. The Lord calls us to our respective vocations, giving grace to each as He deems best for His church (1 Cor. 12:18). He calls one man to be a minister to speak the oracles of God, and another to be a daily worker who serves his employer with the strength God supplies. Both have their place in God's kingdom, and both their duties before God (1 Pet. 4:10–11); both require sacred zeal to answer their callings, for neither can do his work as he should without a heart set ablaze by God.

Consider the typical work environment of a Christian laborer. He is confronted by bad examples; he hears profanity, coarse jokes, and swearing; he is subjected to gossip, slander, complaining, backbiting, · malicious speaking, and lies; he is subjected to office smut that glamorizes sin, expects marriage vows to be broken, and encourages flirting; he is exposed to immodest dress, seductive speech, and wanton eyes. As an employee, he may also be pressured to lie, cheat, steal, deceive, withhold information, or present half-truths as full truths. These pressures encroach on his personal life, his family life, and his spiritual life.

---

8. This section contains a contemporary application of considerable material found on this subject in two Puritan works: Richard Steele, *The Religious Tradesman* (Harrisonburg, Va.: Sprinkle, 1989); Swinnock, "The Christian Man's Calling," in *Works*, vols. 1 and 2, and the first part of vol. 3.

In the company's eyes, nothing is sacred or off limits when financial profits are at stake.

How hard it is for a Christian to obey God in such an environment! Where would the Christian laborer be without sacred zeal? The zealous laborer will give serious consideration to the source, the expectations, and the temptations of his calling.

1. He will be mindful that God is the source of his calling. Though the laborer may at times think he could better serve God elsewhere, and may even prefer to do something else, he trusts that God has placed him where he is. This not only encourages him but also constrains him to be faithful to his calling. He will persevere in the face of adversity when others shrink from it. He will not murmur about his calling but give thanks for it because he knows God's ways are higher than man's ways (Isa. 55:8–9). He trusts that God knows this calling is best for his sanctification, because God is good (Ps. 118:1), will only give him good (Ps. 84:11), and has promised to work out all difficulties for his good (Rom. 8:28). Because God is the source of his calling and the One to thank for his employment, the zealous laborer will do his work not to please men, or to be seen by men, or only when the boss is looking, but rather for the Lord who called him to it (Eph. 6:5–9).

He does everything for the Lord's honor and pleasure; not only his duties, but the way he speaks of his work and how he feels about it. He does his work joyfully, thankfully, and willingly, without murmuring, desiring that since this is the Lord's work, it might become an offering and sacrifice unto God (Eph. 5:2). How great then is the obligation of a laborer's calling!

2. He will be mindful of the expectations of his calling. Having received his calling from the Lord (Eph. 6:5–8), the laborer knows what the Lord requires of him. To be sure, he must follow the orders of his earthly superiors, but as he does so, he is mindful that his work appears before a greater Judge (Acts 4:19; 5:29). Therefore he works with good will "as to the Lord, and not to men: knowing that whatsoever good thing any man doeth, the same shall he receive of the Lord" (Eph. 6:7–8). He also understands that since he is accountable to the Lord as the Searcher of hearts, his internal obedience is just as important as his external obedience, and that the spirit of the law is just as important as the letter (1 Sam. 16:7; Ps. 139:23–24).

Furthermore, he understands that as the Lord's bondservant (1 Cor. 7:22), the expectations of his calling can be summed up in this: that he live to the glory of God (1 Cor. 10:31; Rom. 14:7–8). This is his chief end. It is also his heart's desire. He will be held accountable to this charge for he is not his own, but the Lord's; he has been bought at the highest price, and by the grace of God will live up to it (1 Cor. 6:19–20; 1 Pet. 1:17–19). What great need, then, does the Christian laborer have of Christian zeal!

3. He will be mindful of the temptations peculiar to his calling. Each vocation presents circumstances and opportunities for falling into sin. Some jobs require much travel away from home and family. The laborer must thus spend many nights alone in hotels. Some jobs require many hours of follow-up work on the internet. Some require working closely with people of the opposite sex, whether in person or by phone or by constant e-mail communication. Some require many hours alone in an office. Some require being constantly exposed to the sins of others.

In all of this, the zealous laborer will be mindful of Satan's devices and wiles (2 Cor. 2:11). He will be wary of opportunities and places and situations that Satan might use to set traps of temptation and will be on his guard against them. He will remember that Satan is at war against him and will not miss the least opportunity to destroy him (1 Pet. 5:8). He will guard his ears against conversations that would fill his mind with evil and instead will think only about things that are good (Phil. 4:8). He strives to know his own heart and the temptations to which it is prone (Ps. 139:23–24) and will therefore guard his heart (Prov. 4:23). He will "make a covenant with his eyes" that he will not put any wicked thing before them (Job 31:1; Pss. 101:3; 119:37). He will meditate upon the things of God (Ps. 1:1–3) so that he might always keep himself in the way of God's commandments (Ps. 119:59). He will store up God's Word in his heart so that he might not sin against God (Ps. 119:11).

The zealous laborer will be mindful of his past sins, too, by which the Lord exposed his weaknesses, and therefore will not play with the fire that burned him before. He will refuse to partner with workers of iniquity, but will instead walk before them as a child of the light in hope that God may expose their deeds as evil and bring them to repentance (Eph. 5:6–14). He will be ever mindful that he is never alone; that though he may be anonymous to other men in any given place, he is never anonymous to God and never away from God's all-seeing eye (Job 31:4). He will be mindful that he is accountable to the Lord for all his thoughts, speech, actions, and everything he sets his eyes and affections upon. Most of all, the zealous laborer will be willing, for the sake of his soul and the glory of God, to quit his job if he cannot walk faithfully before his God in it.

Calling #3: The Parent

Of all callings, the role of parent is the most universal and demanding. For though in the Lord's providence some couples remain childless, most are called to parenthood since the covenant blessings have always been and still are to us and our children (Gen. 17:7; Acts 2:39).

As the Christian parent is called to lead his little ones to God, so he must fight against the inherited corruption of their nature, that is, the rebellion in their hearts, their natural aversion to the things of God, and their love of self. Parents realize they must confront the natural wickedness in their children and restrain them from straying into danger. Positively, they must live out their faith in Christ before the watching eyes of their children, and call on them to repent of sin and trust in Him for salvation. They must also be teachers and guides in the way of God's commandments. In all these ways they seek to bring up their children in the nurture and admonition of the Lord.

But all these efforts often seem in vain as instruction appears to fall on deaf ears. Nothing seems to get through to the children's hearts. No wonder many parents feel inadequate for the task committed to them, and are troubled by the thought of the account they will have to give on Judgment Day for the souls of his children. How difficult is this calling!

Not only does the Christian parent have to deal wth the sinfulness of his children, but his ability to carry out his calling is also impaired by his own remaining corruption and actual sin. He has to require from his children the very things he struggles to do himself. He must discipline them for disobedience in the very areas in which he continues to fall into sin. This makes him feel like a hypocrite, nags at his conscience, and weighs heavily on his mind every time he has to correct his children. But overlooking children's sins because as a parent he is wrestling with the same temptations, would only add sin to sin. So he *must* discipline his children.

But worse still, if the children realize they are being disciplined or corrected for the things that their parents appear to get away with, they either complain about a double standard or quietly look forward to the day when they will outgrow such childish rules and can enjoy the sinful privileges and fleshly pleasures that were denied to them as children. How sad if this is truly the case in a Christian home. "Do as I say, not as I do" is a sure way to destroy both ourselves and our children. The Lord reserves His most severe judgments for hypocrites (Matt. 23:13), and for those who sin against the light that they have (Luke 12:47–48).

The daunting task of parenthood is fraught with difficulties and demands self-discipline and self-sacrifice, and a long-term investment of attention and effort. It is the work of many years. What will keep us at the task, year in and year out, in spite of our many failings and discouragements? How shall we persevere without Christian zeal?

The zealous parent will ever be mindful of the gravity, the need, and the promises of his calling. The gravity—the sheer weight of importance—of a parent's calling is inescapable; God holds us accountable for our children's souls. We are stewards of the Lord's heritage (Ps. 127:3), caretakers of the Lord's lambs (Isa. 40:11; John 21:15), and must bring them up according to His instruction and in His nurture, that is, under the means of grace (Eph. 6:4). The basis of our obligation is Deuteronomy 6:4–9, "Hear, O Israel: The LORD our God is one LORD: and thou shalt love the LORD thy God with all thine heart, and with all thy soul, and with all thy might. And these words, which I command thee this day, shall be in thine heart: and thou shalt teach them diligently unto thy children, and shalt talk of them when thou sittest in thine house, and when thou walkest by the way, and when thou liest down, and when thou risest up. And thou shalt bind them for a sign upon thine hand, and they shall be as frontlets between thine eyes. And thou shalt write them upon the posts of thy house, and on thy gates."

A parent's calling is grave because God has appointed Christian parents to be the primary means of training *His* children. Parents stand in God's stead over their children, and children's obedience to parents is rendered "in the Lord" (Eph. 6:1) and is "well pleasing unto the Lord" (Col. 3:20). Furthermore, the gravity of the parents' role is highlighted, as the apostle says, by the fifth commandment, which says, "Honour thy father and mother." This is the first commandment with a promise (Eph. 6:2–3), "that it may be well with thee, and thou mayest live long on the earth" (cf. Ps. 34:12–26). The promise draws a connection between the faithfulness of parents in training their children, and the faithfulness of children in submitting to that training. The future safety and happiness of the individual and the society he lives in depend upon the faithfulness of both parents and children.

John Reynolds said of this great responsibility of parents: "Families are the fundamental seminaries of the world, and of the church.... There devotion should dwell, and an altar be erected, to the eternal God. The zealous parent will present his offspring to the Father of Spirits; will earnestly implore His grace for them, seasonably instill the knowledge of Him, of His Son, and His love to them; and take all care to train them up for the service and enjoyment of Him."[9]

The zealous parent who knows the gravity of his calling will therefore be constrained to practice personal holiness in true repentance. He will strive to live the life to which he calls his children. He will live by faith in the Son of God, and depend upon the grace of God in Christ. He desires that the children may see Christ in him, and in turn may desire the God of their father. He will pursue holiness of life so that he might be an example to encourage his children. He therefore places the

---

9. Reynolds, 177.

highest priority on his walk with Christ, praying that God will use his own relationship with Christ for his children's salvation.

The zealous parent will also manifest true repentance before his children when he sins. He wants them to understand that the war against sin is life-long, and in the battle against sin, a believing parent takes refuge in the Savior to whom he directs his children. He finds the same pardon and cleansing in Christ's shed blood and promise of forgiveness; he enjoys the same comfort in Christ that he holds forth to his children; he proclaims the gospel to them. What the parent seeks to exemplify is not a sinless life of perfection, but a zealous life of faith and repentance, to which the Lord calls him.

The zealous parent will also be mindful of his great *need* of God's transforming grace in his calling. He knows that he cannot so much as move apart from the will and power of God. He cannot find the way, apart from the light of God's Word. He cannot be cleansed of sin and escape condemnation apart from the blood of Christ. He cannot stand upright, or grow in grace apart from the work of the Holy Spirit. So also, He seeks to lead his children to God, but knows this is an impossible task for a human agent, parent, teacher, pastor, or friend. He is fully aware that he must point the way to God and exemplify a walk with God, but only God by His saving power can remove the hard heart of sin and replace it with a heart of flesh (Ezek. 36:26–27), and make his children willing to follow Christ in His day of power (Ps. 110:3).

Aware of his great need of divine grace and the supernatural application of spiritual truths (Zech. 4:6), the zealous parent is compelled to live in prayer. He will daily be on his knees, bringing the lives and needs of his children before the throne of grace (Luke 18:1). He will look to the Lord for the eternal welfare of their souls and plead that his children may come to salvation and become part of the family of God, belonging to the household of Christ for all eternity.

It is true that the parent should strive to be faithful in both discipline and instruction (Eph. 6:4), applying the rod of correction (Prov. 13:24; 22:15; 23:14) and the hand of loving nurture, help, and guidance (Prov. 22:6), for these are parental duties before God. But the zealous parent also knows that only God can crown these efforts with success.

Therefore the zealous parent will make more use of the power of prayer than of the rod of correction, be more in his prayer closet than at his parental lectern, and will talk to God about his children more than to his children about God. He will do so with great perseverance, not here a little and there a little, or now and then, but with constant, persistent, earnest pleading until the Lord answers.

Christopher Love said of such importunity, "It is a gathering together of all the affections of the soul, stirring them all up in prayer, whereby the soul is so earnestly desirous after the good it wants that it will not rest nor leave off the duty until it finds some return."[10] The parent must persevere in prayer (Rom. 12:12) for his children's souls, for the sake of the account he must give of his own stewardship, not letting go of God until He blesses his children (Gen. 32:26). This is the greatest legacy we can leave our children. As Edward Leigh said, "Good parents though they be poor, leave their children a good patrimony [inheritance], for they have laid up many prayers for them in heaven, and they leave them God's favor for their possession; this is urged therefore as a motive by the Holy Ghost to provoke parents unto all righteousness, Deut. 5:29."[11] "The generation of the upright shall be blessed" (Ps. 112:2b).

To that end, a parent will make earnest use of all the means of grace, that is, the ordinances of Christ,[12] the things appointed by God to bring the good news of salvation to his children, as dispensed in public and family worship. He will make sure that his family is in God's house every Lord's Day (Ex. 20:8; Heb. 10:24–25), where they may partake of the blessings of God pronounced upon His people, enjoy the presence of the triune God among His people, witness the grace of God in His people, and learn to sing the praises of God, join in seeking the face of God in prayer, and hear the Word of God read and expounded to His people. Week by week, they will hear that God calls sinners to come to repentance, and promises to save all who come to Him by Jesus Christ (Isa. 55:1–3, 6–7). The parent will ensure that this weekly gospel call rings

---

10. Love, 75–76.

11. Edward Leigh, *A Treatise of the Divine Promises* (London: A. Miller for Henry Mortlocke, 1657), 399.

12. Westminster Larger Catechism, Q. 154.

in his children's ears, trusting that God's Word "shall accomplish that which I please, and prosper in the thing whereto I sent it" (Isa. 55:10–11).

Neither will the parent who depends upon the Lord to touch his children's hearts neglect family worship (Deut. 4:9–10; 6:6–9; Ps. 78:1–7), for he realizes that consistent family worship is just as important as weekly public worship. Therefore he is obligated to God to see that his children have the benefit of both. Daily family worship will consist of Scripture reading and instruction on the portion read, so the Word of God and the good news of Jesus Christ is daily set before the children; of prayers, so that he might teach his children how to pray and encourage them to call upon the name of the God "that hearest prayer" (Ps. 65:2; Isa. 65:24); and of singing, so that his children might learn God's praises and be reminded that God alone is worthy of worship, adoration, and service. Reynolds said that in the home of zealous parents, "sacred zeal...will settle [establish] comely, religious order, and fashion those primitive societies, as nurseries for the Church of God below, and His glorious City above."[13]

Will not the Lord crown such faithfulness, dependence, and importunity? Indeed, He has promised to do so, so He will do it. "Faithful is he that calleth you, who also will do it" (1 Thess. 5:24). Therefore the zealous parent will cherish the divine *promises* that pertain to his calling and be stirred up to trust in the use of God's appointed means. Above all, Christian parents will place their faith in God's Word and anchor their hopes in God's precious promises. Here are some of these sure promises of God:

- God will bless our children temporally because Deuteronomy 7:13 promises that God "will love thee, and bless thee, and multiply thee: he will also bless the fruit of thy womb."

- God will bless our children spiritually because Isaiah 44:3 promises that God will "pour my spirit upon thy seed, and my blessing upon thine offspring," and Isaiah 54:13 promises that "all thy children shall be taught of the LORD; and great shall be the peace of thy

---

13. Reynolds, 178.

children." Leigh wrote, "If we know ourselves to be God's children, we may be assured that some of our posterity shall be so likewise."[14]

• God will bless our children as members of His church. They are heirs of His kingdom and of His covenant, because they are born to Christian parents, and therefore, as the apostle Paul says "they are holy" (1 Cor. 7:14), belonging not to the world, but set apart to God and to His church.

• God will bless our children because He has received them into the visible church by the sacrament of baptism, for He promises, "I will establish my covenant between me and thee and thy seed after thee in their generations for an everlasting covenant, to be a God unto thee, and to thy seed after thee" (Gen. 17:7).

The zealous parent who feels the gravity of his calling, who knows his need for God's grace, and therefore makes diligent use of His appointed means of grace, and who, in the face of difficulty and discouragements, seeks comfort and help in the wonderful promises of God, will not be disappointed, but will enjoy the eternal fruit of his labors (Isa. 55:10–11).

Calling #4: The Private Christian

A person who is not in the ministry, nor a laborer in the workplace, nor a parent, may think that he has no special need for Christian zeal. As Reynolds said, he may think that "he has neither purse nor place, power nor interest, whereby to evidence any zeal for God and religion, [so that] he must be content with a moderate degree of sacred love and piety."[15] Such a view forgets that the Lord who grants greatness to one and lowliness to another commands everyone to be zealous or "fervent in spirit" (Rom. 12:11), zealous in repentance (Rev. 3:19), fervent in prayer (James 5:16), fervent in love for his fellow believers (1 Pet. 4:8), and zealous for the gifts of God (1 Cor. 14:1).

To encourage those who do not have opportunity to express zeal in the ways we have discussed so far, and to provoke those who wrongly conclude that they are of such a low station in life that they are absolved

---

14. Leigh, *Treatise of the Divine Promises,* 398–99.
15. Reynolds, 178.

of the duty to be zealous for the Lord, we suggest several ways in which the private Christian should live in zealous pursuit of the glory of God.[16]

1. The private Christian is to be zealous in prayer. He is to adore God, lifting up hearty praise and thanksgiving to God as the one true and living God. Praise should flow out ("boileth," or "bubbleth up"—KJV margin, n. 4) of his heart as he contemplates the beauty and might of his heavenly King, and makes his tongue the pen of a ready writer (Ps. 45:1).

2. The private Christian is to zealously seek God's kingdom. He is to pray fervently for the peace of Christ's church, and to seek her good (Ps. 122:6–9); and to seek the welfare of the nation, city, and neighborhood he dwells in (Jer. 29:7), as he cries out, "Thy kingdom come. Thy will be done in earth, as it is in heaven" (Matt. 6:9–10).

3. The private Christian will cherish the Lord's chastening (Heb. 12:5) *and be zealous to repent of sin* (1 Cor. 7:11). The zealous Christian sees the loving care and holy purpose of his God in all things. Sacred zeal and love for the Lord will not allow him to misinterpret God's apparent frowns or His adverse providences. Instead, he will cheerfully acquiesce, knowing that all of God's paths are mercy and truth to those who love Him (Ps. 25:10). In particular, he will lovingly submit to God's will in assigning him so lowly a place in the scheme of things. Though he would like to live for the Lord's glory in a more elevated state, sacred zeal will incline him not to complain about his insignificance in the world, but seek to glorify God, though it be in the lowly station of a doorkeeper in the house of the Lord (Ps. 84:10).

Reynolds admitted that cheerful submission is difficult, but he offers encouragement, saying,

> Herein must you submit to divine wisdom and pleasure. Though this perhaps, may be one of the hardest tasks to a zealous soul. The great Disposer of the world must be allowed to call to activity, and call to patience, in an inactive state, whom, and when He pleases. The zealous Elijah must, sometimes, appear before the court and congregation

---

16. Cf. Reynolds, 179–82.

of Israel, busy and intent in God's cause and controversy; and, some-times, must lie still for God, confined in silence and obscurity, where none but ravens shall be his company. The latter scene, probably, cost him the more reluctant submission and self-denial. The good God accepts the will for the deed. And obedience is in his account, better than the fat of rams.[17]

4. *The private Christian should be a witness for God.* Walking by faith, he must follow God's ways and serve Him faithfully in the midst of a rebellious and idolatrous world. By his manner of life, he can be a "liv-ing epistle" (1 Cor. 3:2–3) to people around him, acknowledging God as God, denying himself, bearing his cross, following Christ, walking in love, keeping the commandments, seeking a heavenly country, per-severing to the end. Such a testimony may have a great effect on the consciences of unbelievers.

5. *The private Christian will bear the contempt of his superiors in a Christ-like manner and resist the temptation to raise his circumstances by denying his faith or compromising his integrity.* "We ought to obey God rather than men" (Acts 5:29). "Consider him who endured such contra-diction of sinners against himself" (Heb. 12:3). "It is written of the Son of man, that he must suffer many things, and be set at nought" (Mark 9:12). Reynolds says rightly that the zealous Christian would "rather continue despised and impoverished, than grow wealthy and famous by offending [his] God." This is *sacred zeal* indeed. As Reynolds illustrates, "The Hebrew midwives well discovered their fear of God, and concern for His law, when they consulted not their own safety, by an active obe-dience to the King of Egypt's unjust command."[18]

6. *The private Christian will lament public sin and the dishonor brought to God by the impiety of others.* This sorrow manifests a zeal for the law, authority, and glory of the blessed God and is well pleasing to Him. It is also a way to secure personal peace, if not safety to the land from impending judgments (Ezek. 9:4). Ezekiel 22:30 makes clear that God

---

17. Reynolds, 180.
18. Reynolds, 181.

looked for someone "that should make up the hedge, and stand in the gap before me in the land," that is, as an intercessor, and implies that God's wrath might have been averted had He found one. Did not Abraham show great zeal for the Lord's people by pleading for the righteous who dwelt in Sodom (Gen. 18:22–33)? Thus the private Christian should be zealous to plead with God on behalf of sinful men and nations.

7. The private Christian should zealously pray for deeper communion with the Lord. He draws near to God with love and desire, to behold His beauty and to see His power and glory in the sanctuary (Pss. 27:4; 63:1, 2; 73:28). He will look for every opportunity to glorify God, and long for Christ's return in glory. The zealous soul can cry out in any condition, "Come Lord Jesus, come quickly!" As Reynolds wrote, "Thus, those confined to the most private and retired station have room to exert their zeal and various ways wherein to employ their warm affection for God, His Kingdom, and His glory."[19]

In God's providence, people occupy various stations in life. By discussing the effect of sacred zeal in the minister, the laborer, the parent, and the private Christian, we have attempted to address some of the most important stations that Christians fill in this life. God commands everyone to zealously pursue His glory in all of life, as well as to have zealous faith in His promises, zealous obedience to His commandments, zeal for the good of others, zeal for His cause in the world, and zeal for His approbation on the Judgment Day. Whether the station be high or low, the calling sacred or secular, the duties public or private, every Christian is called upon to do with all his might that which is laid upon him as a calling and task in this life, always relying on God's grace and pursuing the greater glory of His name.

---

19. Reynolds, 181–82.

Study Questions

1. If all Christians were equally zealous, would they all do exactly the same thing? Why or why not?

2. Why did John the Baptist (Luke 3) and Paul the apostle (Titus 2) give different instructions to people of different vocations, ages, and genders?

3. What would be the distinguishing marks of a zealous minister? Who are some models of ministers zealous for the Lord? How did/do they show their zeal?

4. Read 1 Corinthians 15:10. To what did Paul credit his hard work in the ministry? Why should we pray much for the zeal of our ministers?

5. Read Daniel 1:2, 9, 17–19. God is in control of our relocations, relationships with supervisors, and promotions to new responsibilities. How could trusting His providence change our attitude towards our occupations?

6. Read Colossians 3:23–24. What reasons does Paul give to workers to put their heart into their jobs?

7. List some reasons why parents have a high calling and a weighty responsibility. How do these reasons call for zeal in parenting?

8. Edward Leigh said, "Good parents though they be poor, leave their children a good patrimony [inheritance], for they have

laid up many prayers for them in heaven." Why are zealous prayers the best inheritance a parent can give?

9. What would you say to a senior who is not a minister, not in the work force, and not raising children about how he can be zealous for the Lord?

10. Consider each member of your family, according to his or her age, gender, and present vocation in life. What would zeal for the Lord mean for him or her? Pray for the Lord to ignite that person in flaming love to do precisely that.

The Means
to Christian Zeal

Having raised the bar high in our treatment of Christian zeal, many may wonder if such an ideal is actually attainable. We may be tempted to settle for less, but mediocrity, half-heartedness, and lukewarmness are not Christian values. Letting ourselves off the hook with the excuse that the standards set for us are too high is just not an alternative for the followers of Christ.

To curb the tide of lukewarm Christianity, we offer this final chapter on the means to attain and maintain Christian zeal. The zeal of which we have been speaking is not beyond the reach of any saint who sincerely asks it of the Lord and diligently makes use of the means appointed by God for sustaining it. God has called us to burn with sacred zeal. For this Christ has redeemed us. And this zeal alone offers hope for the future of Christ's languishing church (Rev. 2:4–5; 3:2–3, 15–20).

What greater need, then, does the church have in a day of spiritual coolness than to attain this grace? Without it, we are blind to how sinful compromise has stunted our lives and numb to sins that have stolen away our "first love" for God and Christ. Like Lot's wife, we may have succumbed to a fatal attraction for the things we left behind to follow Christ, such as covetousness, lukewarmness in personal devotions, or indulgence in worldly entertainment. Without zeal, we live contrary to our Christian name, contrary to our redemption from sin, contrary to our heavenly citizenship, contrary to our calling to holiness, contrary to our baptism, contrary to our vows as church members, and contrary to our covenant with God, renewed at every celebration of the Lord's

Supper. How can we possibly live "in the world, but not of the world" without Christian zeal? How can we live lives consecrated to God as the first fruits of His harvest of redemption (James 1:18; Rev. 14:4) without Christian zeal? To love God as we should, doing all to His glory, and walk in the light as He is in the light (1 John 1:7), we must be inflamed by Christian zeal.

In speaking of the means to Christian zeal, we will refer to what we must do, with God's blessing, to set our affections ablaze *against* all sinful things and *unto* all holy things. The first and possibly most important thing we must do is to recognize and beware of all the things that hinder and quench the fires of Christian zeal.

Hindrances to Zeal

Nothing so threatens our adversary's territory as sacred zeal, since it is by zeal that our affections are set ablaze for God and against evil. We should not be surprised to find many hindrances to every expression of zeal (Rom. 7:21) and many things which, if tolerated in our lives, will dampen our zeal, and finally quench it.

Beveridge encourages us with these words,

> You are now demolishing the strongholds of Satan, to enlarge the kingdom of Christ. And therefore you can expect no other but the gates of Hell will exert the utmost of their power, and employ all the agents they can get upon earth, to obstruct and hinder it. But that should not slacken your zeal, but make it rather the more flagrant: "for the God of peace will bruise Satan under your feet shortly" [Rom. 16:20]. You fight the battles of the Lord of Hosts, and therefore need not fear what men or devils can do to you. He has often said it, and He will make it good, that all nations shall be subdued to His Son, and be blessed in Him [Pss. 2:8; 22:27; 47:9; 66:4; 72:17; 100:1–2; 117:1; 138:4–5]. Many are so already. And this seems to be the critical time to bring in many more, if not all the rest.[1]

In the presence of such a plenteous harvest, ready to be gathered in (Matt. 9:37, 38; John 4:35), this is indeed a time to be zealous for God.

---

1. Beveridge, "The Duty of Zeal," in *Works*, 6:459.

This is also the time of great opposition, so we must be on our guard against all hindrances to zeal.

1. Speculative religion. Speculative religion is mostly concerned with theoretical and even conjectural questions. William Ames observed: "The intention of the mind about those things which are merely speculative, although it may be a means to find out the truth, yet it hinders the intention of the affections about things practical. And this is the reason why there is more true zeal often found in poor simple Christians, than in our Doctors and Ministers."[2]

Paul warned his young pastors against speculative thinking. He urged Timothy to teach the saints not to "give heed to fables and endless genealogies, which minister questions, rather than godly edifying" (1 Tim. 1:4) and to "strive not about words to no profit," which only ruins listeners (2 Tim. 2:14). Likewise, Paul told Titus to "avoid foolish questions, and genealogies, and contentions, and strivings about the law; for they are unprofitable and vain" (Titus 3:9). Religious speculation may appear to be spiritually mature, but in reality, it hinders the practice of godliness (2 Tim. 3:5). Paul accordingly told Timothy to train himself in practical godliness (1 Tim. 4:7) and strive to present himself to God as a workman who has no need to be ashamed (2 Tim. 2:15). He also reminded Titus that those who believe in God must devote themselves to good works (Titus 3:8).

John Reynolds also viewed speculative religion as a hindrance to zeal because it stifles the experiential nature of Christianity.[3] Christianity appeals to the mind of man with its truths and its written revelation, he said, but does so in order to reach the heart and will of man; it is an experimental religion, not a speculative religion. Therefore people whose Christianity consists of their speculations and ideas tend to be indifferent and lukewarm,[4] for "they that sow sparingly must be content to reap sparingly."[5]

---

2. Ames, 58.
3. Reynolds, 136.
4. Reynolds, 136.
5. Reynolds, 138. Cf. Gal. 6:7.

Christian faith begins with an experiential renovation of the heart (Ezek. 36:26) and progresses by an experiential relationship that impacts all of life. Reynolds explained that the Christian soul, once awakened, "breathes after, and tends towards Heaven, as the perfection and consummation of itself.... They that have *tasted* of this Heavenly Gift, must love that God that imparted it; that holy Word, and quickening Truth, by which it was wrought.... The possessors of this change find such a disposition within them, whereby they are connaturally carried out towards the Holy *God*, the Righteous *Mediator*, and the concerns of *Heaven*."[6] God calls the Christian to converse with Him in prayer, to commune with Him in worship, and to walk with Him in all of life. Can mere religious speculation produce such an experiential life? Can mere talk about religious things lead to a life of faith and good works? Indeed not. As Reynolds said, "They that are strangers to such experience, how can it be expected, that they should be warm for religion, and the way of it?"[7] Beware, then, of religious speculation that fails to lead you in the way of practical holiness (James 1:22–25).

2. The love of the world. How can we be zealous for heaven when our hearts are wrapped up in earthly things? How can we lift our spirits heavenward when our minds are weighed down with the cares of this life? How can we be zealous for God when our love is divided between Him and this world? Worldly mindedness will starve our zeal.[8] The thorny "cares and riches and pleasures of this life" (Luke 8:14) will choke our zeal for God and prevent us from bearing fruit.[9] Christ said, "No man can serve two masters: for either he will hate the one, and love the other; or else he will hold to the one, and despise the other. Ye cannot serve God and mammon" (Matt. 6:24)? How can we be zealous for the Lord if we give him only half of our love and loyalty?

Besides, in embracing the world we embrace God's enemy (1 John 5:19) and thereby make *ourselves* God's enemy (James 4:4). Worldly

---

6. Reynolds, 136–37.
7. Reynolds, 139.
8. Reynolds, 145.
9. Ames, 58.

mindedness can only cool our affections for heavenly things. Samuel Ward warned that the love of the world would put out the love of the Father. He said, "They cannot stand together in intense degrees, one cannot serve both these masters with such affection as both would have. Seldom do you see a man make haste to be rich, *and* thrive in religion.... As you love zeal, beware of resolving to be rich, lest *gain* prove thy godliness; take heed of ambitious aspiring, lest courts and great places prove ill airs for zeal.... Peter, while he warmed his hands, cooled his heart.... If you are willing to die poor in estate, you may the more easily live in grace."[10]

Beware, then, of loving this world. A covetous mind, like that of Demas (2 Tim. 4:10), will oppose, starve, and finally quench Christian zeal, which is marked by self-denial (Mark 8:34), dying to the world (Gal. 6:14), and the willingness to spend and be spent for God and His truth (Phil. 2:17–22).[11]

3. Spiritual presumption. Sometimes such a presumption is nothing more than "carnal security," one of "the usual effects of rash presumption or of idle and wanton trifling" with the doctrine of election (Canons of Dort, Head I, Article 13). Having made a beginning in the Christian faith, some people assume they have done all they need to do, that election guarantees their salvation, and they can devote themselves to pursuits of their own. Others suppose that God only calls us to put off gross public sins; having done so, we need not worry about the private and secret sins of the heart. Many subscribe to the notion that in this life we can attain to a level of "Christian perfection," or "victorious living," or "fullness of the Spirit," so that we no longer have to battle against sin and strive for holiness; in fact, such people sometimes claim they no longer sin at all.

None of these notions squares with Scripture's testimony. Rather, the apostle Paul says in Philippians 3:13–14, "Brethren, I count not myself to have apprehended: but this one thing I do, forgetting those things which are behind, and reaching forth unto those things which

---

10. Ward, 84. Italics ours.
11. Reynolds, 145.

are before, I press toward the mark for the prize of the high calling of God in Christ Jesus." If the apostle Paul, under divine inspiration, could say that we are to follow or "imitate" him as he followed Christ (1 Cor. 11:1; Phil. 3:17), considering himself still in the race and still pressing forward with holy zeal towards the prize, then who in the entire church of God can rightly suppose that he has achieved perfect obedience, where he no longer needs zeal? "No, but even the holiest men, while in this life, have only a small beginning of this obedience."[12] Beware, then, of spiritual presumption. We must not cease striving until our bodies lie resting in the grave, when our souls are received into the highest heavens, and made perfect in holiness.[13]

4. Neglect of the means of grace. When we presume that we no longer need to gird up our loins (1 Pet. 1:13), lay aside every weight and every besetting sin, and run the race set before us (Heb. 12:1–2), we will naturally neglect those means that God has appointed to keep our zeal burning. Zeal will grow so cold that it will inevitably die out.[14] To neglect the means of grace is to neglect the fuel that feeds this spiritual fire. We must beware of neglecting anything that God has given us to help us grow in Christ-likeness. To neglect these means is to weaken ourselves as Christians, and put everything at risk.

5. Impenitence. Ward wrote, "Gross sin every man knows will waste the conscience, and make shipwreck of zeal. But I say, the least known evil unrepented of, is as a thief in the candle,[15] or an obstruction in the liver…. Zeal and sin will soon expel the one or the other out of their subject. Can you imagine in the same roof God and Belial, the ark and Dagon?"[16] Impenitence with regard to any known sin will surely quench all zeal for God.

---

12. Heidelberg Catechism, Q. 114.
13. Westminster Confession, 32.1.
14. Ward, 83.
15. A "thief" in a candle was a piece of burnt wick which falls down into the melted wax and hinders the flame.
16. Ward, 84.

David knew what it felt like to have his zeal for God quenched by impenitence: "When I kept silence, my bones waxed old through my roaring all the day long. For day and night thy hand was heavy upon me: my moisture is turned into the drought of summer" (Ps. 32:3–4). While he continued in sin, he had no comfort, and daily felt the ebbing away of all spiritual life. So also in Psalm 38:3, he says, "There is no soundness in my flesh because of thine anger; neither is there any rest in my bones because of sin." The exercise of his great gift of song and singing was taken away (Ps. 51:14–15).

By God's grace, David turned to the Lord and poured out his heart, confessing his sin and begging to be forgiven and cleansed. The Lord forgave his transgression and covered his sin (Ps. 32:1, 5), restoring to David the enjoyment of his comfort in Christ ("blessedness," v. 1; "compassed about with mercy," v. 10) and his gift of song ("compassed about with songs of deliverance," v. 7). David then called upon the godly to pray to the Lord while He might be found and to avoid the misery that he had so foolishly and needlessly suffered by persisting in unrepented sin. Beware, then, and keep short accounts with God, who has promised to forgive us our sins as often as we confess them (1 John 1:9). It is foolish to continue in sin when the fountain of cleansing grace ever flows (Heb. 10:4–5, 10, 14), and the righteous Advocate ever intercedes for us, as our High Priest (1 John 2:1–2; Heb. 7:25).

6. *Indulgence in any known sin.* When we indulge ourselves in any known sin, or absolve ourselves of any known duty, how can we avoid the charge of hypocrisy in condemning the sins and failings of others (Rom. 2:17–24)? Do we think that God is pleased with our crying down the sins of others while we commit the same sins? Do we imagine that God is pleased when we accuse others of failure, while we excuse ourselves from the very same duties? As we said before, "Do as I say, not as I do" is a poor substitute for observing all things whatsoever the Lord has commanded.

Sacred zeal reaches to *all* of God's commandments and *all* of Christian duty. Thus zeal is extinguished by the quench-coal of known sin.[17]

---

17. Ward, 84.

There is no more sure way to quench the Holy Spirit (Eph. 4:30). If we would keep a fire in our heart for God, we must take caution not to indulge in any known sin, or neglect any known duty.

7. Indifference and unbelief. Reynolds said this enemy is the "bane of sacred zeal."[18] It is not enough to have an interest in religious questions, an understanding of basic religious doctrine, or even a small stock of memorized Scripture verses, if all this fails to touch the heart, because out of the heart, as Solomon said, flow the issues of life (Prov. 4:23). An unmoved, indifferent heart will not give rise to zeal. Light in the head must be matched by warmth in the heart. To change a person, divine truths must be "pressed upon the soul by potent consideration and sound belief."[19] How many people have listened to powerful sermons from Christ's ambassadors who beseech them to be reconciled to God, only to go home untouched by all appeals and arguments, and quick to fall asleep upon the pillow of their sins? Why is such warm preaching lost upon such cold people? They are indifferent to what they hear, and receive nothing with faith in the heart, and so they remain "unprofitable hearers" and "hearers of the word, and not doers" (James 1:22–24). Of such hearers, Reynolds wrote,

> Were the mind convinced, we might expect the heart would be warmed. But we see that *impiety* still abounds. Practical *atheism* and infidelity are still rampant. Religion is but a name to some; is cold in the best. It is a sign [that] faith is weak or asleep....
>
> Did we by faith discern the presence and inspection of the blessed *God*, did we see the power and love of the *Mediator*, sat down at the right-hand of God, did we see the *attendants* and *joys* of the celestial world, how ashamed should we be of all our deadness and lukewarmness! But our unbelief spoils all! *I have believed, therefore I have spoken,* says the psalmist, and after him, the apostle [2 Cor. 4:13]. Could we believe, we should speak, and live, and act, at another rate than we do now. Faith would kindle, and love would be diligent and unwearied in the service of God and His Christ.[20]

---

18. Reynolds, 134.
19. Reynolds, 134.
20. Reynolds, 135–36.

One of the great reasons for the lack of zeal for the Lord is failure to believe the great truths of the gospel which we have in Christ, and indifference with regard to the duties that Christ requires of us. Beware then, of the presence and influence of any lingering unbelief and indifference in your heart.

8. *Ignorance.*[21] We learned in the first chapter that the second mark of Christian zeal is knowledge imparted by the light of divine truth. How can we be zealous for the things of God if we dwell in the darkness of ignorance about divine truth? Reynolds said, "Holy knowledge must kindle *sacred zeal*; knowledge of those things that are the proper objects of it. They are incomparably charming and attractive. Some things indeed are made the matter of strict disquisition, that, upon examination, do but cheat the search and study. An insight into them quite sinks their price and value; but others there are, that want only to be known, that they may captivate, and inflame the soul; and such are the great things of the Christian religion."[22]

He asked, "What holy fire from the altar would be dropped into our souls, were we vouchsafed such a vision [as Isaiah had], or a suitable knowledge of [God]? But our darkness and distance chills our hearts and powers, and prevents the sacred zeal that should spring and flourish there."[23] We therefore must strive to banish ignorance, and to "grow in grace, and in the knowledge of our Lord and Saviour Jesus Christ" (2 Pet. 3:18). If we persist in ignorance of "the knowledge of God, and of Jesus our Lord" (2 Pet. 1:2), our comfort must speedily diminish, and our zeal will soon give way to indifference of heart and languor of spirit.

9. *Cowardice.*[24] We cannot advance God's cause in the world if we fail to be bold for Him. Sin will comfortably abide in our churches unless it is put out by great boldness. Hypocritical professors will continue to bring shame to the name of Christ unless exposed by great boldness.

---

21. Reynolds, 131.
22. Reynolds, 132.
23. Reynolds, 134.
24. Reynolds, 142.

The ministry of prayer will languish if we do not come boldly to the throne of grace. Sinners will not repent and believe if we do not preach the Word with all boldness. We live in the days of which the apostle warned, "when they will not endure sound doctrine; but after their own lusts shall they heap to themselves teachers, having itching ears; and they shall turn away their ears from the truth, and shall be turned unto fables" (2 Tim. 4:3–4). Such a day cannot be endured without zeal. As Paul charged Timothy, "But watch thou in all things, endure afflictions, do the work of an evangelist, make full proof of thy ministry" (v. 5). Without zeal, Timothy could not have endured the hardships of the ministry, persevered in his call to preach, or fulfilled his ministry among people. It was boldness that convinced religious leaders in Jerusalem that the unlearned and ignorant disciples "had been with Jesus" (Acts 4:13). Such boldness in ordinary men set ablaze by the Spirit of God (v. 8), was the fruit of sacred zeal.

Yet, how many Christians are bold for Christ? How many are able to bear reproach for Christ's cause? How many shrink back when they should stand and fight (Eph. 6:10–11; Heb. 10:39)? Reynolds lamented,

> How unworthy and unfit are we to be witnesses for God, in an untoward, revolting generation? We cannot bear a reproach, a taunt, a wry mouth, a jest or sneer, or any of those silly slights, wherewith ill natured, and ill mannered fools treat the professors of piety.
>
> We have scarce composure of face enough, now a days, to sustain the gravity and solemnity of religion. Persons (and pretended worshippers) must now enter the sacred assemblies, as airy and unconcerned, as if they attended an *Opera*. They must make an ostentation of all their gaiety, as if they came to act in a scene. They must seem loose and negligent in their devotions, least they should be thought in good earnest, in what they are about. They must gaze, and whisper, and smile in time of sermon, lest they be thought seriously attentive to the Words of wisdom.
>
> And then an unserious people infects the ministry; and they must be ashamed too, of the due exercises of their function. They must learn to speak smooth and soft, lest they touch their hearers' hearts. They must pronounce the most awful, weighty things with a nice, cursory turn, lest their words make too deep an impression, or they should be thought solicitous for souls. They must be afraid or ashamed of detaining gentle ears too long, though they are reporting to them things

worthy to be heard by both ears. They must meditate short discourses, run over prayer in haste, because they must be ashamed of what hairbrained fops will call long prayer and long preaching.[25]

If we test ourselves by the standards Reynolds applies, how many of us must confess that we have stumbled over this hindrance to Christian zeal! We have all been guilty of cowardice; many of us have long ago laid down our weapons, and put off our armor and waved the flag of surrender, as the captors and prisoners of our own cowardice.

Where is that inextinguishable zeal of the apostle who was willing to be imprisoned for the Lord Jesus and even to die for Him (Acts 21:13)? Are we not indwelt by the same Spirit who filled both Paul and the Lord Himself (Rom. 8:9–11)? Will not that Spirit grant us the boldness of a lion to oppose all unrighteousness and stand our ground in duty (Dan. 3:17ff.)? Indeed He will. Remember the three Hebrew young men (Dan. 3), threatened by Nebuchadnezzar with death in the fiery furnace, boldly declaring that, "our God whom we serve is able to deliver us from the burning fiery furnace, and he will deliver us out of thine hand, O king. But if not, be it known unto thee, O king, that we will not serve thy gods, nor worship the golden image which thou hast set up" (Dan. 3:17–18). Trusting in God, they resolved to do their duty at all costs.

Consider another example. When Jeremiah cried out to God because of all he had suffered as God's prophet, and asked the Lord to defend him, the Lord responded, "Let them return unto thee; but return not thou unto them. And I will make thee unto this people a fenced brasen wall: and they shall fight against thee, but they shall not prevail against thee: for I am with thee to save thee and to deliver thee, saith the LORD" (Jer. 15:19–20). Jeremiah was told not to fear the people nor give way to cowardice, but to stand his ground; trusting that the Lord would be with him, making him a "brasen wall" against which the people could not prevail. In other words, the Lord did not promise to lessen the opposition of the people, but to fortify the prophet against it. Thus fortified, Jeremiah went back to the task of speaking the Word of the Lord with all boldness.

---

25. Reynolds, 143–44.

John Owen said that divine protection not only keeps us safe against the world but it also actually encourages our religious zeal. He said this protection is

> the best defense against opposition; and that not a weak, tottering wall, that might easily be cast down, but a brazen wall, that must needs be impregnable. What engines can possibly prevail against a wall of brass? And to make it more secure, this brazen wall shall be fenced with all manner of fortifications and ammunition; so that the veriest coward in the world, being behind such a wall, may, without dread or terror, apply himself to that which he finds to do. God will so secure the instruments of His glory against a backsliding people, in holding up the ways of His truth and righteousness, that all attempts against them shall be vain, and the most timorous spirit may be secure, provided he go not out of the Lord's way.... And, indeed, who but a fool would run from the shelter of a brazen wall, to hide himself in a little stubble?... It is a sure word, and forever to be rested upon, which the Lord gives in to Asa, 2 Chron. 15:2, "The Lord is with you, while ye be with him."[26]

We must not give way to cowardice, for the Lord has called us to stand our ground and not be afraid. He has promised to be with us and to strengthen us against all opposition. He has also promised to uphold us and enable us, that we may obey Him fully. Therefore let us "be strong in the Lord, and in the power of his might" (Eph. 6:10). Let us regard all opposition and assaults of the enemy, not as hindrances, but rather as whetstones for our fortitude, and occasions to put our trust in the Lord. As Ward said,

> They that mean to take the kingdom of God by violence, provide themselves to go through fire and water, carry their lives in their hands, [and] embrace [flaming logs]; they say to father and mother, 'I know you not,' to carnal counselors and friendly enemies, 'Get you behind me, Satan.' Zeal is as strong as death, hot as the coals of juniper, floods of many waters cannot quench it. Agar [Prov. 30:29–31], speaks of four things, stately in their kind; I will make bold to add a fifth, comprehending and exceeding them all, namely the zealous Christian; [he is as] strong and bold as the lion, not turning his head for any; as swift as the greyhound in the ways of God's commandments, in the

---

26. John Owen, "Righteous Zeal Encouraged by Divine Protection," in *The Works of John Owen* (Edinburgh: Banner of Truth, 1991), 8:149–50.

race to heaven; as nimble as the goat, climbing the steep and craggy mountains of piety and virtue; [and as] a victorious king, overcoming the world and his lusts; Solomon in all his royalty is not clothed like [a zealous Christian] in his fiery chariot.[27]

The Means for Attaining Christian Zeal

Recognizing the hindrances of Christian zeal is the first of many important things we must do to maintain this sacred grace. We must not neglect these other means if we would be zealous for the Lord.

1. Prayer. True zeal is the gift of God and must be sought in prayer. Ward said, "Say not in your heart, What Prometheus shall ascend into heaven and fetch [this fire] thence? You may fetch it thence by your own prayer, as did Elias and the apostles, men of infirmities as well as yourself. Pray continually and instantly. The Lord that breathed first your soul into you, will also breathe on your soul. Prayer and zeal are as water and ice, mutually producing each other."[28]

We are not to wonder how so great a grace can be ours, as if we must do something great to qualify for it, or as though there is some great difficulty to be overcome to acquire it. Thankfully, Jesus Christ has indeed won this gift from the hand of God, and all other things that pertain to life and salvation. Consequently, zeal is acquired the same way we obtain all other graces and gifts of God, namely, by asking for it in Jesus' name, trusting that "God will give His grace and Holy Spirit to those only, who with sincere desires continually ask them of Him, and are thankful for them" (Heidelberg Catechism, Q. 116). Luke 12:32 says that it is the Father's good pleasure to give us the kingdom, and Luke 11:13 promises us that the Father will give the Holy Spirit, and all His good gifts, to those who ask Him.

The chief thing that stands in the way of our receiving this gift is our failure to ask for it. James 4:2 says, "Ye have not, because ye ask not." What stands in the way of our asking for zeal is unbelief—zeal's great

---

27. Ward, 79.
28. Ward, 81–82.

enemy. If we sincerely yearn to be inflamed with zeal, we must humble ourselves before God, believing His Word to be true. We must acknowledge our need and His bounty, confessing our sin and His mercy. We must ask Him, for the sake of the Lord Jesus, to enliven our affections and inflame our hearts by the light of His Word and work of the Holy Spirit, that we may "begin to live not only according to some, but all the commandments of God," hating all sin, delighting in all righteousness, and doing the things He commands for His glory, for our comfort, and for the salvation of others.

Some will scoff at this, saying praying for zeal is too easy, while others will say it is too hard and murmur against it. These critics will never possess true zeal because they refuse to take God at His word. Others, though equally undeserving, and perhaps by nature reserved and undemonstrative, will have their affections stirred and their hearts inflamed with holy zeal because they believe Him who has promised and humble themselves to ask (Heb. 11:6). For as Luke 11:9–10 says, "Ask, and it shall be given you; seek, and ye shall find; knock, and it shall be opened unto you. For every one that asketh receiveth; and he that seeketh findeth; and to him that knocketh it shall be opened."

Just as prayer obtains zeal, prayer also maintains it. The neglect of prayer will quickly put out the fire of zeal. Ward said, "If a man forbear his accustomed meals, will not his natural heat decay? The Levites that kept God's watch in the temple, were charged expressly, morning and evening, if not oftener, to look to the lights and the fire. He that shall forget (at the least) with the curfew-bell in the evening to rake up his zeal by prayer, and with the day-bell in the morning to stir up and kindle the same, if not oftener, with Daniel; I cannot conceive how he can possibly keep fire in his heart. Will God bless such as bid him not so much as good-morrow and good-even?"[29] Can any of us expect to be aflame for God if we neglect the simple means of prayer? Certainly not. Neglect of prayer will very quickly cool our zeal.

---

29. Ward, 83.

2. God's Word. Another means of maintaining zeal is the public ministry of the Word of God. Ward said, "When [the fire of zeal] is once come down upon your altar, though no water can quench it, yet must it be preserved fresh by ordinary fuel, especially the priest's lips must keep fire alive. Sermons are bellows ordained for this purpose."[30]

Later Ward asked, "He that shall despise or neglect prophecy, must he not needs quench the Spirit?"[31] The preaching of the Word is a powerful means of blowing on the coals of zeal and keeping them aflame because God Himself speaks in the sermon. When the Word is faithfully preached, God speaks through it to our hearts. He lights His match, then blows upon our coals with His Spirit, causing our zeal to burn afresh.

Likewise, the faithful reading of the Scriptures feeds our zeal by pouring fuel on the holy fire in our bosom. Ward wrote, "After the sparkles once by [prayer and sermons are] kindled, cherish and feed them by reading the word. Let it dwell richly in your heart."[32] The Word feeds the zealous love for God which He graciously places in our hearts. Would we have this love cool and this zeal die out? Then we must not neglect to fuel it. Would we have this seed of grace come to full fruition in every area of our lives? Then we must cultivate it to full bloom.

3. Meditation. We must meditate often upon the love and mercy of God towards us,[33] that though we were His enemies by nature (Eph. 2:1–3), He still loved us and sent His Son to redeem us (Rom. 5:8–10). We must also meditate upon our daily imperfections,[34] for though we are dead unto sin and alive unto God (Rom. 6:11), we are yet plagued with a loathsome tenant—our old nature—who mixes poison into our every offering (Rom. 7:21–23). We should meditate upon God's all-seeing eye[35] and remember that God minds all our ways and counts all our steps (Job 31:4). He knows the way we walk and hears the words we say. He looks into our hearts and knows our thoughts. We should think

---

30. Ward, 82.
31. Ward, 83.
32. Ward, 82.
33. Ames, 59.
34. Ames, 59.
35. Ward, 82.

also about the deep pit from which God dug us and the great height to which He has lifted us, that we who were but worms of sin (Ps. 22:6) have now been seated with Christ in the heavens at God's right hand (Col. 3:1–3). We should often bring to mind that Christ came to this world and died to purchase us as a people who would put off all sin and be zealous for good works (Titus 2:11–14).[36] We should remember that our God is a consuming fire and a jealous God who hates lukewarmness (Rev. 3:15–16). We should consider God's judgments against hypocrisy (Isa. 1:11–15) and His great aversion to the commingling of sin and solemn assembly.

We should also remember that in the fires of affliction the Lord chastens those He loves; He will keep us under affliction until our dross in consumed.[37] We should meditate often upon our future estate in heaven, considering how thankful we will one day be of our zeal, yet how paltry our zeal really is, compared to its gracious issue and the incomparable glories of heaven. We will one day proclaim from heaven that, had we known what God had in store for those who served Him with fervent zeal, we would have heated up our zeal seven times hotter than it was. Such meditations will ensure that the fire of zeal will not go out in us but will burn brighter with each passing day.

4. Public Worship. Public worship provides the ideal context for the dispensing of the means of grace. In addition to prayer and the ministry of the Word, public worship also affords us the opportunity to sing God's praises, confess our faith, receive God's blessing, encourage our fellow believers, and be encouraged by them. Hebrews 10:24–25 commands us not to neglect public worship, saying, "let us consider one another to provoke unto love and to good works: not forsaking the assembling of ourselves together, as the manner of some is; but exhorting one another: and so much the more, as ye see the day approaching." Gathered for worship, we can exhort one another to stay the course (James 1:12), run the race (1 Cor. 9:24), fight the fight, keep the faith (2 Tim. 4:7), and not shrink back (Heb. 10:39). In the assembly we put the interests of others

---

36. Ward, 82.
37. Ward, 82.

above our own (Phil. 2:3–4) and urge each other to press on to maturity in Christ (Phil. 3:12), to lay hold of the prize for which Christ laid hold on us (Phil. 3:14), and to hold true to what we have attained (Phil. 3:16). Surely the coal of zeal, which would quickly cool if left alone, will burn brighter, hotter, and longer when kept amidst others.

How detrimental, then, is the neglect of these several means of grace. Ward wrote, "Such as read the Bible by fits upon rainy days, not eating the book with John, but tasting only with the tip of the tongue; such as meditate by snatches, never chewing the cud and digesting their meat, they may happily get a smackering, for discourse and table-talk, but not enough to keep soul and life together, much less for strength and vigor. Such as forsake the best fellowship, and wax strange to the holy assemblies (as now the manner of many is), how can they but take cold? Can one coal alone keep itself glowing?"[38] The hottest zeal will quickly cool without the use of God's appointed means![39]

Keeping the Right Perspective on Zeal

Admittedly, both the means to attain Christian zeal and the means to keep it aflame may seem weak. If we consult the wisdom of men, then we may think that there must be something else, something more demanding, something more within the scope of what we can do to ourselves and for ourselves. Think of Naaman the leper (2 Kings 5). When Naaman came to Elisha to be healed of his leprosy, he expected the prophet to treat his case with the methods of the ancient shaman or "medicine man," with a ritual invocation and imposition of hands. When Elisha merely sent a messenger to Naaman telling him to wash himself in the Jordan River seven times, Naaman went away in a rage. What was the Jordan compared to the great rivers of Damascus (v. 12)?

Naaman's faith was not in Jehovah as the God of Israel, nor in the prophet Elisha as His servant and spokesman. His faith was placed in

---

38. Ward, 83.

39. Other means that could be expounded on here include exercising communion of saints, reading sound literature, maintaining spiritual journaling, engaging in evangelism, and practicing stewardship.

the means that he expected the prophet to use. Once Naaman's servants pointed out the foolishness of Naaman's unwillingness to use the simple means prescribed for him, and demanding something else (v. 13), Naaman humbled himself and submitted to the word of God. Verse 14 says, "Then went he down, and dipped himself seven times in Jordan, according to the saying of the man of God: and his flesh came again like unto the flesh of a little child, and he was clean."

Likewise, if we consider the means to Christian zeal in light of our own wisdom and judge them by our own standards, we will be no less foolish than Naaman. But if we consider them in light of God's wisdom and God's hands, then everything changes. To God, a stone is not too small to slay a giant (1 Sam. 17:40), a few loaves and fish are not too little to feed thousands (Mark 6:38), and a company of three hundred is not too few to slay an army of tens of thousands (Judg. 8:10). "God hath chosen the foolish things of the world to confound the wise; and God hath chosen the weak things of the world to confound the things which are mighty; and base things of the world, and things which are despised, hath God chosen, yea, and things which are not, to bring to nought the things that are: that no flesh should glory in his presence" (1 Cor. 1:27–29). If we believe God's promise that such means are not frail but mighty through God, devoting ourselves to using them with all faith, diligence, and self-denial, then we will receive the grace to put off our lukewarmness and be set ablaze with sacred zeal.

The means of grace are also meant to compel those around us, not to praise and admire us, but to give glory to God (Matt. 5:16). If we could acquire zeal (or any other grace) by our own efforts or using means of our own devising, then we would never give thanks or glory to God, but would instead take pride in ourselves and boast in our own strength (Luke 12:16–20). As 1 Corinthians 1:21 says, it has pleased the Lord to save those who believe by the foolishness of preaching; so it has pleased the Lord to give zeal to those who deny themselves and humbly ask for it, and to keep it aflame in those who diligently use the means which He has appointed.

May God therefore humble us by our lack of zeal for Him and the advancement of His glorious kingdom, and cause us to despise and cast off our lukewarm Christianity. May He humble us by showing us how helpless we are to dispel our coolness and make ourselves burn for Him, how prone we are to embrace moderation, and how quickly and easily our affections cool. But may He also hear our prayers for zeal, inflaming our hearts with holy affections, that we may be fervent in spirit, steadfast in prayer, bold in speech, and bold in our obedience to Christ.

A Final Appeal

We began this book with John Reynolds's lament about the lack of zeal among the Christians of his day. Let us now close with his appeal for sacred zeal in all of Christ's church:

> May we agree to consider the words of that great Primate [leading bishop], the late Archbishop of York...: "O what a world of good may we all do, if we had a true zeal of God! How many occasions and opportunities are there put into our hands, every day (in what condition and circumstances soever we are) which, if we were acted by this principle, would render us great benefactors to mankind, by discouraging vice and impiety, and promoting virtue and goodness in the world?"
>
> Could we agree in the exercise of such a beneficent principle, how happy would our [world] be? But if we must not act by that principle in concert together, yet let us act by it notwithstanding. If we must stand divided and separate still, yet let us put on zeal for God and His Kingdom among men! Let us ardently love the *Lord Jesus*, and the affairs of His redemption and glory! Let us be serious and diligent in all the offices of a truly *sacred zeal*![40]

May God bless this study on Christian zeal so that its truths may not be choked or uprooted in us, but come to full fruition, giving way not only to resolutions to be zealous for God but to persevere in using the appointed means so that we may always be zealous for our God. As Revelation 3:19 says, "Be zealous!"

---

40. Reynolds, 184–85.

Study Questions

1. William Ames said that "speculative" religion, that is, religion only in the head, is one reason "why there is more true zeal often found in poor simple Christians, than in our Doctors [teachers] and Ministers." What are the signs of mere head knowledge?

2. Read Luke 8:14. How do the cares of this world affect the fruitfulness of the Word in us? How do we detect and resist worldliness so that it does not drain our zeal?

3. Read Philippians 3:13–14. What is the opposite of resting proudly upon your past attainments? What does it mean to "press on" towards Jesus Christ?

4. Why would tolerating "small" sins quench your zeal? How should we deal with such violations of God's law if we want to fan into flame our love for the righteous God?

5. Reynolds said, "Were the mind convinced, we might expect the heart would be warmed." Give some examples of biblical teachings such that if we believed them with all our hearts, we would be moved to flame with zeal. How do we overcome unbelief?

6. The fear of man brings a snare (Prov. 29:25). How does cowardice before men dampen our zeal for the Lord? What can we do when we fear man?

7. Read Luke 11:11–13. Why can we be confident that the Father will give us more of the Spirit's fire if we pray for it? What does the comparison to children needing food teach us about how we should pray for the Spirit's work in us?

8. Reynolds said, "Holy knowledge must kindle sacred zeal." Once God lights the spark of love in our hearts, how can we keep fueling it with the knowledge of God?

9. Read Psalm 143:5–6. When David was grieving, how did he stir up his soul to thirst after God? What practical steps can you take to set your mind thinking upon God?

10. Why does our zeal tend to cool when we do not regularly join the saints in worship? How has God used the public worship of the church to renew your zeal?

Selected Readings
on Christian Zeal

Adams, Thomas. "Heaven Made Sure; or, The Certainty of Salvation." In *The Works of Thomas Adams*, 1:60–70. Edinburgh: James Nichol, 1861.

Ames, William. "Of Zeale." In *Conscience with the Power and Cases Thereof*, 56–60 [book 3, ch. 6]. N.p., 1639.

Annesley, Samuel. "How May We Attain to Love God with All Our Hearts, Souls, and Minds?" In *Puritan Sermons, 1659–1689*, 1:517–621. Wheaton, Ill.: Richard Owen Roberts, 1981.

Bates, William. "Spiritual Perfection Unfolded and Enforced." In *The Whole Works of the Rev. William Bates*, 2:289–526. Harrisonburg, Va.: Sprinkle Publications, 1990.

Beveridge, William. "The Duty of Zeal. A Sermon Preached before the Society for the Propagation of the Gospel in Foreign Parts, at the Parish Church of St. Mary-le-Bow, Feb. 21st, 1707." In *The Theological Works of William Beveridge*, 6:447–61. Oxford: John Henry Parker, 1845.

Bowles, Oliver. *Zeale for Gods House quickned: or, A sermon preached before assembly of Lord, Commons, and Divines, at their solemn fast Iuly 7, 1643*. London: by Richard Bishop for Samuel Gellibrand, 1643.

Brooks, Thomas. "The Unsearchable Riches of Christ." In *The Works of Thomas Brooks*, 3:54–55. Edinburgh: Banner of Truth, 2001.

Evans, John. "Christian Zeal," Sermon XVIII. In *Practical Discourses Concerning the Christian Temper.* London: for C. and R. Ware, T. Longman, and J. Johnson, 1773.

Flavel, John. "A Treatise of the Soul of Man." In *The Works of John Flavel,* 3:214–16. Edinburgh: Banner of Truth, 1968.

Greenham, Richard. "Of Zeal," a sermon from "Seven Godlie and Frvit-fvll Sermons Vpon Svndry Portions of Holy Scripture." In *The Workes of the Reverend and faithfvll servant of Iesus Christ, M. Richard Greenham, Minister and Preacher of the word of God,* 113–20. London: Imprinted by Felix Kingston for Ralph Iacson, 1599.

Hopkins, Ezekiel. "Exposition upon the Commandments." In *The Works of Ezekiel Hopkins,* 1:275–76. Morgan, Pa.: Soli Deo Gloria, 1995.

Jenkyn, William. *An Exposition upon the Epistle of Jude,* 104. Minneapolis: James & Klock, 1976.

Love, Christopher. *The Zealous Christian: Taking Heaven by Holy Violence in Wrestling and Holding Communion with God in Importunate Prayer.* Repr., Morgan, Pa.: Soli Deo Gloria, 2002.

Manton, Thomas. Sermon XXII, "Zealous of Good Works," from "Sermons upon Titus ii. 11–14." In *The Complete Works of Thomas Manton,* 16:275–92. London: James Nisbet, 1874.

Murray, Iain H. "The Puritans on Maintaining Spiritual Zeal." In *Adorning the Doctrine,* 72–94. London: Westminster Conference, 1995.

Owen, John. "Righteous Zeal Encouraged by Divine Protection." In *The Works of John Owen,* 8:133–62. Edinburgh: Banner of Truth, 1991.

Reynolds, John. *Zeal a Virtue: or, A Discourse Concerning Sacred Zeal.* London: Printed for John Clark, 1716.

Sibbes, Richard. "The Faithful Covenanter." In *The Works of Richard Sibbes,* 6:10–13. Edinburgh: Banner of Truth, 2001.

Swinnock, George. "The Christian Man's Calling, Part I." In *The Works of George Swinnock*, Volumes 1, 2, and first part of 3. Edinburgh: Banner of Truth, 1992.

Ward, Samuel. "A Coal from the Altar to Kindle the Holy Fire of Zeal." In *Sermons and Treatises*, 69–91. Edinburgh: Banner of Truth, 1996.

Watson, Thomas. *Heaven Taken by Storm: Showing the Holy Violence a Christian is to Put Forth in the Pursuit after Glory*. Ed. Joel R. Beeke. Morgan, Pa.: Soli Deo Gloria, 1992.